OSPREY COMBAT AIRCRAFT • 61

F-16 FIGHTING FALCON
UNITS OF OPERATION
IRAQI FREEDOM

SERIES EDITOR: TONY HOLMES

OSPREY COMBAT AIRCRAFT • 61

F-16 FIGHTING FALCON UNITS OF OPERATION *IRAQI FREEDOM*

STEVE DAVIES & DOUG DILDY

OSPREY
PUBLISHING

Front cover
At midday on 2 April 2003, Lt Chad Martin, flying F-16CG Viper 90-0744 of the 524th Expeditionary Fighter Squadron (EFS)/332nd Air Expeditionary Wing (AEW), took off from Al Jaber AB, Kuwait, on his second CAS mission of the day. He and his flight lead, Capt Charles Davis, were tasked with destroying Iraqi Army ground defences surrounding Baghdad International Airport with 500-lb GBU-12 laser guided bombs (LGBs).

Establishing a 'wheel' orbit at 20,000 ft overhead the target area, Davis quickly destroyed several munitions storage bunkers while Martin provided cover. The latter, following his flight lead in a 30-degree cone at his 'six o'clock' some one to three miles behind, was on the lookout for any SAM launches or other threats opposing the formation. During one of his last attacks Davis spotted Iraqi tanks ensconced in earthen revetments, and quickly destroyed one.

Now Martin began to eliminate other targets, picking his aim points carefully, rolling in on them in a dive, locking on the AAQ-14 LANTIRN pod and releasing the LGB, followed by a sharp pull off-target and a climb back up into the 'wheel' pattern. Using this tactic, Martin destroyed three more Iraqi tanks before Bingo fuel forced the flight to return to Al Jaber. For this mission Davis and Martin were awarded the USAF's Distinguished Flying Cross (DFC).

Martin subsequently recalled;
'I remember that mission the most not because I got the DFC for it, but because it put all of the things I had achieved in OSW/OIF together for me. I was responsible for my Flight lead's safety, and actually had to be directive. I used my training and tools successfully, took out some tanks and saw the fruits of our labour by watching V Corps roll into Baghdad International on Fox News before I went to bed that night. It was gratifying knowing that I had played a small part in helping them to do that' (*Cover artwork by Mark Postlethwaite*)

First published in Great Britain in 2006 by Osprey Publishing
Midland House, West Way, Botley, Oxford, OX2 0PH
443 Park Avenue South, New York, NY 10016, USA

ISBN 1 84176 994 0

Edited by Tony Holmes
Page design by Tony Truscott
Cover Artwork by Mark Postlethwaite
Aircraft Profiles by Chris Davey
Scale Drawings by Mark Styling
Index by Alan Thatcher
Originated by United Graphics, Singapore
Printed and bound in China through Bookbuilders

06 07 08 09 10   10 09 08 07 06 05 04 03 02 01

For a catalogue of all books published by Osprey please contact:
NORTH AMERICA
Osprey Direct, C/o Random House Distribution Center,
400 Hahn Road, Westminster, MD 21157
E-mail:info@ospreydirect.com

ALL OTHER REGIONS
Osprey Direct UK, P.O. Box 140 Wellingborough, Northants, NN8 2FA, UK
E-mail: info@ospreydirect.co.uk
www.ospreypublishing.com

ACKNOWLEDGEMENTS
The authors would like to thank the following individuals for their help with this book – Cols Stanley Clarke and Scott Manning, Lt Cols David Kossler, William Sparrow, Pete Schaub and Scott Patten, Majs Brian Wolf, Anthony Roberson, Bernie Yosten, Paul Griggs and 'Bear' McAtee, Capts Chad Martin, Tad Clark, Mark Johnson, Steve Strandburg, Paul Carlton, Jared Patrick, Gene Sherer, Jason Cochran, Matt Renbarger, Ryan Peterson, Dave Rogers, Kenzie Jones, Tim Cole and Jason Medina, Lts Gerardo Gonzalez and Suzanne Ovel, MSgts Sean Cobb, Jerry Stroud and Anthony Skipworth, TSgts Jim Elmore, Kathleen Cordner and 'Bull' Kelly, SSgts Prakash and Heather Kraft, SFC Katherine Perez, SrA Cynthia Schlegel, Niels Boman, Jon and the team at www.f-16.net and Scott Brown at www.afterburnerdecals.com.

CONTENTS

F-16 OVERVIEW

Perhaps the first thing that any reader should know about this aeroplane is that despite its officially-sanctioned title Fighting Falcon, the F-16 actually goes by the monicker Viper. In a world where the importance of looking, acting and sounding cool cannot be over-exaggerated, fighter pilots who fly the F-16 know it by no other name. With that small, but decidedly important, clarification out of the way, here's a brief overview of the jet.

The F-16 was originally conceived as a light weight, short-range point defence fighter to complement the McDonnell Douglas F-15 Eagle. First introduced into service in 1978, the F-16 has since benefited from a succession of upgrades identified in 'Blocks' (Block 10, Block 25 etc.), as well as major overall airframe improvements that manifest themselves as marks (F-16A, F-16C etc.).

The F-16A covered Blocks 1-20, and was superseded by the F-16C, which began at Block 25. The latter featured the AN/APG-68(V) radar, a 'glass cockpit' consisting of two Multi Function Displays (MFDs), a wide-angle Heads Up Display (HUD), up-front controls, support for infrared (IR) video, increased-capacity environmental control and electrical power systems, a MIL STD-1760 data bus/weapons interface, allowing the employment of AGM-65D Maverick and AIM-120 AMRAAM (Advanced Medium Range Air to Air Missile), improved fire control and stores management computers and a Have Quick II anti-jam UHF radio.

Blocks 40 and 50/52 F-16Cs were used by the United States Air Force (USAF) in Operation *Iraqi Freedom* (OIF) in March 2003, and Block 30s were employed by the Air National Guard (ANG).

FROM VIPER TO 'WILD WEASEL'

It was during the latter years of the Vietnam War that the USAF introduced the first truly sophisticated Suppression of Enemy Air Defence (SEAD) fighters, most notably the F-100F Super Sabre and the F-105F/G Thunderchief. A rapid proliferation of Soviet-supplied surface-to-air missile (SAM) sites across North Vietnam had rendered the *Iron Hand* mission, which had typically concentrated on destroying anti-aircraft artillery (AAA) emplacements, largely impotent. With specialist mission equipment for hunting and killing SAMs a prerequisite, the 'Wild Weasel' was born. Various iterations of the F-105F/G were seen, and many

The YF-16 Light Weight Fighter was the prototype of what would become known as the Viper. Originally designed as a VFR day fighter, the F-16 would move on to become an accomplished all-weather, day and night, multi-role fighter (*General Dynamics*)

Taking over the 'Wild Weasel' role from the F-4G was no small task, and although the decision to retire the 'Rhino' remains a contentious one in some circles, the F-16CJ Block 50/52 has certainly risen to the challenge (*FJPhotography.com*)

lessons were learned, before the archetypal SEAD platform – the F-4G Phantom II – was finally born. Viewed by many as the most potent SAM killer ever, the F-4G performed with alacrity during the 1991 Gulf War, after which it was promptly retired from service, much to the chagrin of many a seasoned 'Wild Weasel' crew. Its successor was the F-16CJ.

The version of the Viper chosen for the SEAD role was the F-16CJ Block 50D/52D, which was then one of the latest versions of the airframe, and the only one powered by the Pratt & Whitney F-100-PW-229 (Block 52) and General Electric F-110-GE-129 (Block 50) Improved Performance Engines (IPE). The standard Block 50 airframe features GPS navigation, a Ring Laser Gyro Inertial Navigation System (RLG INS), an AN/ALE-47 threat-adaptive countermeasures system and a Horizontal Situation Display (HSD), which is a digital moving map over which flight, weapons, target and navigation data can be laid. The jet also boasts Night Vision Goggle-compatible cockpit lighting and the AN/APG-68V(5) radar, which offers improved reliability and detection ranges over previous versions. Combined, these modifications give the aircraft a significant boost in performance in both air and ground arenas.

Taking the standard Block 50D/52D F-16C and upgrading it to perform the SEAD role involved the addition of two main pieces of mission-specific equipment. The most obvious of these is the AN/ASQ-213 HARM Targeting System (HTS), which is a small pod affixed to the right side of the intake cheek. It is used to find, classify, range and display threat emitter systems to the pilot. This information in turn allows the pilot to cue the AGM-88B/C High speed Anti-Radiation Missile (HARM) to specific threat systems.

Introduced into service in order to provide an enhanced all-weather capability by day or night, the F-16CG Block 40/42 boasts the intake-mounted AAQ-13 navigation and AAQ-14 targeting pods, which combine to form LANTIRN (*Lockheed Martin*)

Supplementing the all-important HTS are the AN/ALR-56M advanced Radar Warning Receiver (RWR), AN/ALQ-131(V)14 Electronic Counter Measures (ECM) pod and additional underwing-mounted chaff dispensers to complement those already mounted on the lower rear fuselage adjacent to the horizontal stabilisers.

The second key component unique to the F-16CJ is the Avionics Launcher Interface Computer

(ALICS), which resides in the AGM-88 HARM launcher pylon and acts as the conduit between the HTS, the Central Computer and the missile itself. Pronounced 'a-licks', the ALICS is essential for successful hand-off of radar threats from the jet to the HARM.

A close up of the AAQ-14 targeting pod reveals the mounting configuration on the cheek of the F-16CJ's intake (*USAF*)

NIGHT STRIKERS AND GUARD VIPERS

The Block 40 F-16C is equipped for enhanced all-weather and night capability. It carries the LANTIRN (Low Altitude Navigation Targeting IR for Night) navigation and targeting pods, features a holographic HUD, automatic terrain following capability, a pressure breathing system to improve G-tolerance, an enhanced envelope gunsight and a moving ground target bombing capability, in addition to many of the improvements seen in the Block 50/52. To top it off, the airframe was strengthened to expand the 9g flight envelope from 26,900 lbs gross weight to 28,500 lbs. Maximum take-off weight was also increased to 42,300 lbs, which, combined with the need to provide adequate ground clearance for the two LANTIRN pods, prompted new undercarriage struts that were not only of heavier construction, but also physically longer. Bulged landing gear doors accommodate the larger wheels and tyres that are associated with the heavier ground handling loads of the Block 40.

The Block 30/32 F-16 was the first Viper variant to feature a common engine bay able to accept either the Pratt & Whitney F100-PW-220 (Block 32) or General Electric F110-GE-129 (Block 30). The F110 produces 5000 lbs more thrust than the F100, and requires a larger amount of air, prompting the redesign of the F-16's inlet to satisfy this requirement. Early F-16C/D Block 30s have 'small inlets', but F110-powered Vipers from F-16C 86-0262 onward feature the aptly-coined 'big-mouths' – the official name for this modification is the 'modular common air intake duct'. The Pratt & Whitney Block 32 F-16s all have the smaller inlet, which is referred to as a 'normal shock inlet'.

In order to satisfy the requirement for multi-target capability, the AIM-120 was added to the F-16's arsenal in the Spring of 1987, prompting the designation Block 30B. Expanded memory was provided for the Programmable Display Generator and the Data Entry Electronics Unit. Block 30/32 also introduced the Seek Talk secure voice communication system, and these jets were equipped with seal-bond fuel tanks.

In August 1987 provisions to fire the AGM-45 Shrike and AGM-88 HARM were made, together with installation of a voice message unit and crash-survivable flight data recorder. Block 30D introduced twice as many chaff/flare dispensers and moved the forward RWR antennas to the leading edge flaps. Dubbed 'beer can' antennas for obvious reasons, these have since been retrofitted onto all previous F-16C/Ds.

READYING FOR WAR

Quietly ensconced within the 32nd Air Operations Group (AOG) at Ramstein AB, in Germany, Maj Anthony 'Roby' Roberson was in the middle of his tour with USAF Europe (USAFE) when, in 2002, US President George W Bush gave the order to start planning for the invasion of Iraq. Mired in controversy to this day, the decision was made ostensibly as a result of Iraq's inability to account for the whereabouts of its chemical weapons. Iraq's dictator, Saddam Hussein, flouted a spate of United Nations' resolutions, and with Great Britain backing the US unflinchingly, war became a certainty.

An experienced F-16 pilot and Weapons Instructor Course graduate, 'Roby' was assigned to the 32nd AOG after recently completing a frontline tour in the F-16CJ. He checked into Ramstein in June 2002, nine months before the war commenced;

'I was involved in OIF well before it actually started. Stationed in Germany, I was the division chief for combat plans.'

Roberson's remit was to provide a fighter pilot's impetus to the creation of the plan, and his expertise in F-16 operations meant that he was closely involved in allocating Viper units to the theatre, and in defining their role in the overall plan;

'The first part of the planning was that from the outset we wanted to fight a multi-front, joint campaign. Our operations were very limited from the north, and the majority of the air component's forces were based in the south. So, right up front, it wouldn't take a rocket scientist for the Iraqis to work out where the main thrust of our attack would have to come from.'

Here, Roberson was referring to the creation of two fronts in OIF – the southern front, for which aircraft would be based at airfields in Saudi Arabia and Kuwait, and the northern front, which consisted of aircraft operating from Incirlik AB, in Turkey. 'We didn't want a south-centric campaign – there's more risk to forces if you don't have the opportunity to surprise', he added.

With the first objective out of the way, Roberson concentrated on the other key campaign objectives, which included the complete removal of Saddam's regime. Supported by experts from the holistic airframes and mission design series (MDS), Roberson set to work creating a plan that would allow USAFE to deliver on its commitments to the joint plan.

'We had the first 30 days planned 90 days before the war started. Normally, the first 72 to 96 hours are re-planned time and time again. It's easy to plan in the vacuum of air operations only, but remember that when H-hour began, we were going to have Special Operations Forces (SOF) inserted into the west, the critical take down of oil platforms in the

Arabian Gulf, V Corps Marine Expeditionary Force that was anxious to bolt out of Kuwait and lots of other things that had to be considered.'

Roberson planned to an excruciating level of detail – 'What bomb, on what target, at what time', he said. The resulting Joint Air Operations Plan for the air component provided all the phasing for the air war, of which a small segment pertinent to each day was isolated to create the Air Tasking Order (ATO) – the document from which every MDS in-theatre would draw its daily taskings, targets, tanker assignments, times over target, weapons loads and fusing.

F-16 UNIT ASSIGNMENTS

The first priority of OIF would be to take control of the battle space, necessitating an extensive SEAD effort to remove key individual components of Iraq's integrated air defence system (IADS). This would

Both F-16CJ squadrons from the 52nd FW at Spangdahlem AB, Germany, deployed to OIF. Initially set to be located at Incirlik AB, Turkey, they were eventually deployed to Al Udeid AB, Qatar, when Turkish basing rights were refused (*FJPhotography.com*)

The 77th FS 'Gamblers' from Shaw AFB, South Carolina, was earmarked to be the lead unit of the 363rd AEG (*FJPhotography.com*)

require F-16CJs, alongside Navy and Marine Corps EA-6B Prowlers and F/A-18 Hornets, to work in a coordinated fashion to achieve this singularly important goal.

The USAF commitment to this objective was spearheaded by the F-16CJs of the 77th FS/20th FW from Shaw AFB, South Carolina. The 'Gamblers' were earmarked to deploy to Prince Sultan Air Base (PSAB), Saudi Arabia, where they would be the dominant squadron in the 363rd Air Expeditionary Group (AEG). The 363rd would also be home to eight Block 50 F-16CJs of the 14th FS/35th FW from Misawa AB, Japan, six Block 40 F-16Cs of the 4th FS/388th FW from Hill AFB, Utah, and six Block 30 F-16Cs of the USAF Reserve-manned 457th FS/301st FW from Luke AFB, Arizona. Roberson recalled that combined, these F-16s were tasked with 'defence of the battle space and other aircraft'.

The 20th FW's advance party arrived at PSAB in the early hours of 13 February 2003, and were immediately engulfed in a sand storm of great ferocity – it was an environmental phenomenon that the squadron would soon grow accustomed to.

Two days later, six 77th Expeditionary Fighter Squadron (EFS) jets joined those of Misawa's 14th FS, which was already in-theatre for its routine three-month Operation *Southern Watch* (OSW) No-Fly Zone rotation. Six other Shaw F-16CJs were stuck at Moron air base, in Spain,

Above left and above
Additional SEAD support at PSAB would come in the shape of eight F-16CJs from the Misawa-based 14th FS/35th FW and six F-16C Block 40s from Hill AFB's 4th FS/ 388th FW. These aircraft were assigned the 'defence of the battle space' mission (*USAF*)

Seen firing an AGM-65 Maverick missile in peacetime conditions, the 'CC' tail codes identify this jet as an F-16C of the 524th FS/27th FW from Cannon AFB. The 'Hounds' received orders to deploy eighteen Block 40 Vipers to Al Jaber, Kuwait, as part of the 332nd AEG (*USAF*)

with mechanical difficulties, but they joined the fray a day later on 16 February. These 12 aircraft would later be augmented by four more jets, bringing the total to 16 F-16CJs. As well as additional airframes, the 'Gamblers' also borrowed pilots from the 55th and 67th FSs, which remained at Shaw AFB. This brought the pilot ratio up to two pilots per jet, and also drafted some valuable experience into the unit's ranks.

The F-16CG-equipped 524th FS/27th FW from Cannon AFB, New Mexico, was tasked with sending 18 Block 40 jets to Al Jaber AB, Kuwait, as part of the 332nd AEG. Like the 14th FS in Saudi Arabia, the 524th FS 'Hounds' had deployed into the theatre in December 2002 as part of AEF VII for OSW. Twelve jets initially deployed, and another six arrived later when the unit 'plussed-up' for seemingly inevitable hostilities. Roberson explained that the squadron was 'put there to provide us with alert and interdiction capabilities, being a part of the air defence plan for Kuwait'.

It would be the 524th's job to scour the border between Iraq and Kuwait, providing non-traditional information surveillance and reconnaissance (NTISR) intelligence on border activities or incursions. The squadron's F-16CGs were also identified as being key platforms from which M129 leaflet dispensers would be dropped as part of an expansive psychological warfare effort in the final weeks of OSW.

Perhaps the most important mission – politically, at least – was assigned to 410th Air Expeditionary Wing (AEW). The latter was comprised of the Alabama ANG as the lead wing, plus Vipers from the Colorado and Washington DC ANGs and a contingent of Air Force Reserve (AFRES) F-16Cs from the 466th FS/419th FW, based at Hill AFB, Utah. The 160th FS/187th FW, Alabama ANG had some of the most capable F-16s in the Air Force, as we shall later see.

The Block 30 Vipers of Colorado's 120th FS/140th FW and Washington DC's 121st FS/113th FW would use their finely-honed reconnaissance skills to help the Alabama F-16Cs hunt for Scud missiles in what was called, simply, anti-TBM (Theatre Ballistic Missile) missions. Amidst great secrecy, the US State Department negotiated a bed down base for the group in Azraq, Jordan. From this Royal Jordanian Air Force fighter base, the four squadrons would patrol the western deserts of Iraq, whilst tacitly providing simultaneous support to SOF troops conducting the same mission on the ground.

In keeping with the concept of co-locating aircraft types with similar roles, the Royal Air Force (RAF) assigned a small contingent of Harrier GR 7s and a pair of Canberra PR 9 reconnaissance platforms to the same base. Roberson referred to an 'Anti-TBM umbrella' when discussing the activities of the 410th AEW in western Iraq.

The fourth, and final, F-16 deployment had been planned to bed down at Incirlik, Turkey, in order to accomplish the multi-front plan which Roberson and his superiors had been so keen. When last-minute negotiations between Turkish officials and the US State Department failed to yield an agreement, however, Roberson was ordered to relocate these forces to the southern front. F-16CJs of the 52nd FW's 22nd and 23rd FSs duly departed Spangdahlem AB, Germany, for Al Udeid AB, in Qatar. Spangdahlem's 71st FS A-10s and F-15Es of the 48th FW's 492nd and 494th FSs, based at RAF Lakenheath, England, were cancelled from OIF altogether.

The 379th AEW to which the 'Spang' F-16CJs were assigned was also home to identical jets from the 157th FS/169th FW, South Carolina ANG (SCANG). The three 'CJ' units were assigned SEAD, Destruction of Enemy Air Defences (DEAD), Time-Sensitive Targeting (TST) and Close Air Support (CAS) as their primary missions. The 22nd FS deployed 12 jets – a mixture of their own, and some from sister squadron, the 23rd FS – on 17 January, which was 12 years to the day since the first Gulf War commenced. They were joined in February by the 23rd FS, which brought with it a further 12 CJs (both 22nd and 23rd FS jets).

The 22nd FS aircrew arriving at Al Udeid were initially delayed from flying while diplomatic permissions were negotiated with the Qatari representatives, although these were secured eventually.

During the in-processing briefing at Al Udeid, a Qatar Emiri Air Force colonel who was also a Mirage 2000-5 pilot briefed the local area procedures. He is reported to have said, 'You listen to me talk, or you no fly in Qatar. I am good pilot, trust me. We can zoom up to 40,000 ft'. One F-15E Weapons System Officer present in the room told the author, 'the funny part was seeing the dudes from the 22nd EFS sitting in the front row behaving themselves while this guy was talking, and then the quote came, "De Meer-aage two-thousand Daash five is excellent airplane, much like your American F-16 in many ways . . . Just better!" At the time we Strike Eagle guys snickered, but you could actually hear the F-16 guys roll their eyes'.

In response, the 22nd EFS CO sitting at the front is rumoured to have crossed his legs, thus exposing the sole of his flying boot, and simultaneously given the colonel the thumbs up signal, both of which are considered an insult in Qatari culture!

OSW – THE FINAL DAYS

All four units now in-theatre began flying OSW sorties in the same manner that most F-16 pilots had experienced during their previous three-month tours to the region. OSW had no offensive objective beyond curbing and discouraging the illegal incursion of Iraqi Air Force (IrAF) fighters into the UN-mandated No-Fly Zones, but with war imminent, these missions were used to fine-tune key skills – night flying, for example – as well as to fly NTISR sorties for the purposes of gathering intelligence on the disposition and whereabouts of the Iraqi military machine. The F-16CJs did this through the use of the HTS, 'sniffing the air' for telltale electrons that might give away the location of a previously unnoticed SAM or AAA system. The Block 30s and 40s used their IR target pods to good effect in the visual spectrum, too.

NTISR was misunderstood by some of the CJ pilots according to Maj Roberson. 'To ask someone to do something outside of what they have planned to do requires a different mindset. For a Block 52 guy to be told, "I want you to fly to this destination and 'take a picture' of this, then come back and show it to me", would seem to most fighter pilots a total waste of time. They didn't think it was an effective use of their capabilities, and at that point in time the value of this mission was misunderstood'.

In fact, these sorties provided Gen Michael Moseley, Ninth Air Force Commander and boss of Central Command's air component, with a valuable picture of the electronic order of battle. Roberson continued,

Left and below
Despite the fact that OIF would be fought by units deployed to the south of Iraq, Vipers based out of Incirlik continued to fly NTISR sorties until 19 March, 2003. Here, the 55th EFS – a unit of the 27th FW from Shaw AFB – flies one of the very last ONW sorties (*USAF*)

'it is critical for an F-16CJ to be able to swing to that role and use its array of pods to get pre-strike reconnaissance, thus providing coherent change detection – something that was there yesterday is not there today. We needed to get that information back into the analysts' hands so that they could tell us what the adversary was doing. The Viper is a good platform for this tasking'. The NTISR sorties were usually pre-planned, but Roberson tasked several time-critical NTISR sorties to airborne F-16s.

Indeed, there was a significant NTISR effort ongoing in western Iraq involving the 410th AEW's 'F-16C+s' (an unofficial designation given to ANG Vipers equipped with the AAQ-28 Litening II target pod), the first sortie of which had been planned personally by Roberson. In addition to gathering intelligence on TBM activities, this effort was almost certainly geared to gathering vital intelligence for punitive strikes that would in turn pave the way for SOF operations when OIF commenced.

Mapping Iraq's Early Warning (EW) radar networks and observation posts was critical because they would give Iraq advance warning of the infiltration of SOF troops flying in aboard fixed- and rotary-wing aircraft from Jordan.

The AAQ-28 Litening II pods issued to the 160th FS Alabama ANG resulted in the squadron unofficially redesignating its jets 'F-16C+s'. The pods were just one of several improvements made to the unit's jets prior to its deployment to Jordan. Four pilots also visited Nellis AFB, Nevada, to practise Scud hunting with the pod (seen here installed on an F-15E) (*FJPhotography.com*)

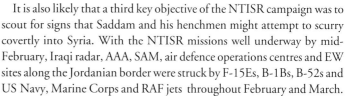

It is also likely that a third key objective of the NTISR campaign was to scout for signs that Saddam and his henchmen might attempt to scurry covertly into Syria. With the NTISR missions well underway by mid-February, Iraqi radar, AAA, SAM, air defence operations centres and EW sites along the Jordanian border were struck by F-15Es, B-1Bs, B-52s and US Navy, Marine Corps and RAF jets throughout February and March.

The ANG Vipers had trained extensively to accomplish the NTISR mission prior to their deployment. They had placed a particular emphasis on practising finding, identifying and killing the TBMs that would almost certainly be targeted at nations friendly to the Coalition – particularly Israel. Accordingly, in late 2002 a small detachment from the 160th FS visited Nellis AFB, Nevada, where it had worked with the Weapons School and practised the techniques and procedures that would later be used in combat. The detachment then returned to the 160th's Montgomery-Dannelly Field base and disseminated its findings to the rest of the squadron's pilots.

The information being collected and the targets being struck almost nightly in punitive attacks by a range of Coalition aircraft types were all leading to the preparation of the battlefield pre-OIF. The name for this escalation from punitive attacks to all-out war was OPLAN 1003V, which defined how the Coalition would initiate full-scale ground- and air-operations to unseat the Iraqi dictatorship. It was derived from OPLAN 1003-98, which was the 1998 'off-the-shelf' defence plan should Iraqi forces once again attempt to occupy Kuwait.

In keeping with its tasking to defend the battle space, and other aircraft, F-16CJs of the 77th EFS/363rd AEG also flew SEAD escort

Below and bottom
F-16CJs of the 77th EFS provided SEAD escort for a series of intelligence-gathering U-2 flights in OSW. Although these missions were generally quiet, there were several close calls when F-16s cycling to and from the tanker came close to midair collision.
(**USAF and Lockheed Martin**)

missions in the final days of OSW. Lt Col Scott Manning was the squadron's Assistant Director of Operations, and he flew his first OSW sortie on 21 February. Three days later he lead the SEAD escort force for a single U-2 reconnaissance aircraft as it skirted the Baghdad SuperMEZ (Missile Exclusion Zone), from which his HTS and HARM missiles detected only a few emissions.

On 28 February Manning flew another U-2 escort mission, noting in his diary, 'The flight path took us as far west as Jordan and close to the Syrian border. Again, the mission was very quiet'. He concluded that Saddam was keeping his SAMs off-air in an attempt to 'look good in the eyes of the world'. On 5 March Manning was nearly killed when he came close to colliding with his flight lead during a night U-2 escort mission;

'During the second refuelling between tanker operations and NVG transition, I had a very close call with "Rowdy". We pulled off the tanker in a right-hand climbing turn and it was pitch black. "Rowdy" rotated his light switch to "off". Having been watching him in the right turn, I could not see that he had stopped his turn. I, however, stayed in my right turn while perceiving him to still be in his.

'In retrospect, I should have rolled out and called for his lights. Instead, I stayed in the turn and reached up to pull my goggles down. I heard the blast of the mighty GE-129 pass right over my canopy, at which point I looked up to the left (keep in mind I am still in my right turn), only to see "Rowdy" now out on my left side, and only about 20 ft away. I was fortunate that he had looked at me during this and pulled back on his stick to let my aircraft pass underneath him.'

The irony of the situation was not lost on Manning as he signed-off his diary. 'The "official war" has not started, yet we could have lost two aircraft and quite possibly suffered a mortality or two'. Saddam's SuperMEZ might have been quiet thus far, but mistakes of even a simple nature could be just as deadly in the high-risk business of fast jet flying. The four PSAB Viper units continued to fly escort, NTISR and Defensive Counter Air (DCA) missions up until the first night of OIF.

Spangdahlem's F-16CJs, now bedded down and packed in like sardines on Al Udeid's rapidly overcrowding ramp, also flew force protection missions for F-15E, F-16CG, F-14, F/A-18 and B-1B aircraft tasked with striking IADS, leadership, logistics and other key targets within Iraq as part of OSW. Iraqi resistance to these pre-war strikes was light, and as far as can be ascertained the 22nd EFS fired only a single AGM-88 during this time. Official squadron records show that the 23rd EFS flew 129 OSW sorties prior to OIF, accounting for 654.8-hours of combat flying time. All four F-16CJ squadrons – the 22nd, 23rd and 77th EFSs and the 157th FS – were also flying on-call SEAD '24/7'.

19 March saw the phased changeover from OSW to OPLAN 1003V. At 0300Z the Airspace Coordination Order changed, switching over the routes, altitudes and names used to enter Iraqi airspace and altering the location of the tanker tracks. At 1800Z the Special Instructions (SPINS) changed, significantly altering the rules of engagement (RoE), and where and how Coalition aircraft could fly. Shortly thereafter, an F-15E dropped the last-ever OSW bomb, guiding a GBU-28 laser-guided bomb (LGB) into the Intercept Operations Centre at H3 air base.

Things were about to get very serious indeed.

COLOUR PLATES

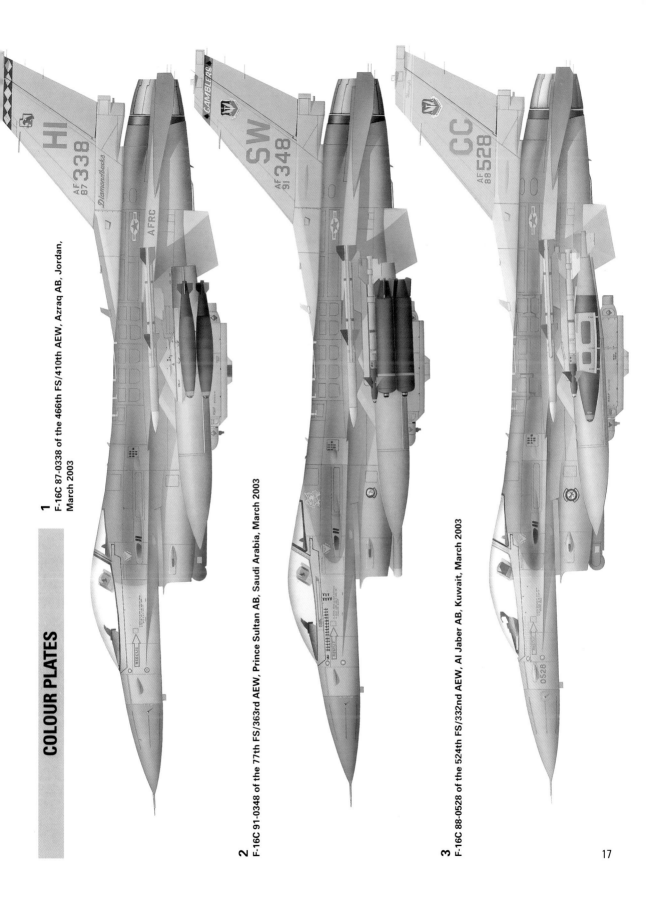

1
F-16C 87-0338 of the 466th FS/410th AEW, Azraq AB, Jordan, March 2003

2
F-16C 91-0348 of the 77th FS/363rd AEW, Prince Sultan AB, Saudi Arabia, March 2003

3
F-16C 88-0528 of the 524th FS/332nd AEW, Al Jaber AB, Kuwait, March 2003

4

F-16C 90-0776 of the 524th FS/332nd AEW, Al Jaber AB, Kuwait, March 2003

5

F-16C 94-0042 of the 77th FS/363rd AEW, Prince Sultan AB, Saudi Arabia, March 2003

6

F-16C 92-0920 of the 77th FS/363rd AEW, Prince Sultan AB, Saudi Arabia, March 2003

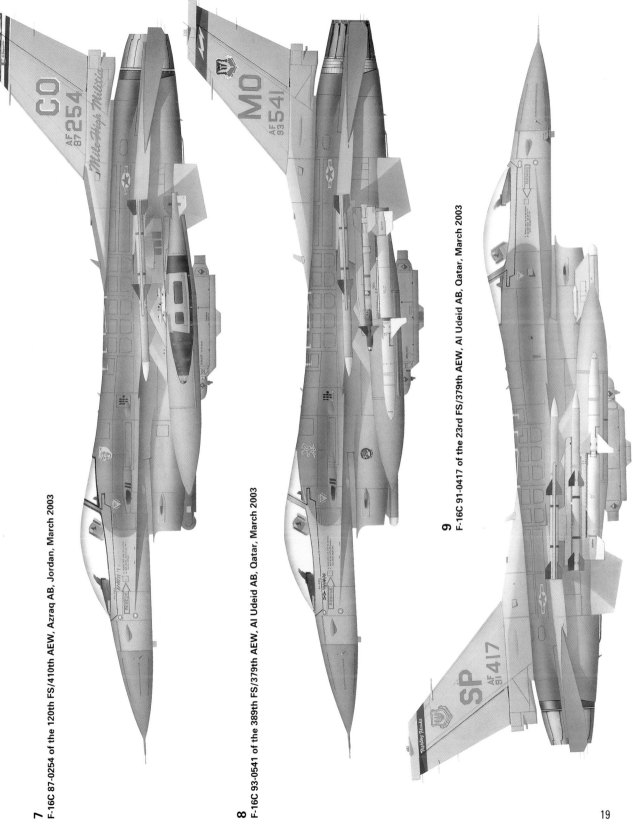

7
F-16C 87-0254 of the 120th FS/410th AEW, Azraq AB, Jordan, March 2003

8
F-16C 93-0541 of the 389th FS/379th AEW, Al Udeid AB, Qatar, March 2003

9
F-16C 91-0417 of the 23rd FS/379th AEW, Al Udeid AB, Qatar, March 2003

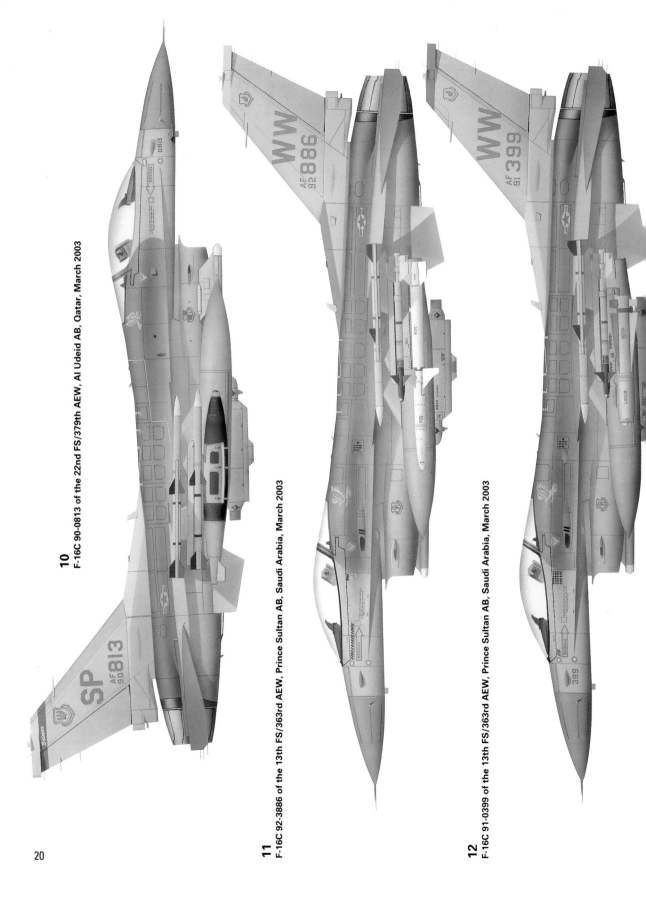

10
F-16C 90-0813 of the 22nd FS/379th AEW, Al Udeid AB, Qatar, March 2003

11
F-16C 92-3886 of the 13th FS/363rd AEW, Prince Sultan AB, Saudi Arabia, March 2003

12
F-16C 91-0399 of the 13th FS/363rd AEW, Prince Sultan AB, Saudi Arabia, March 2003

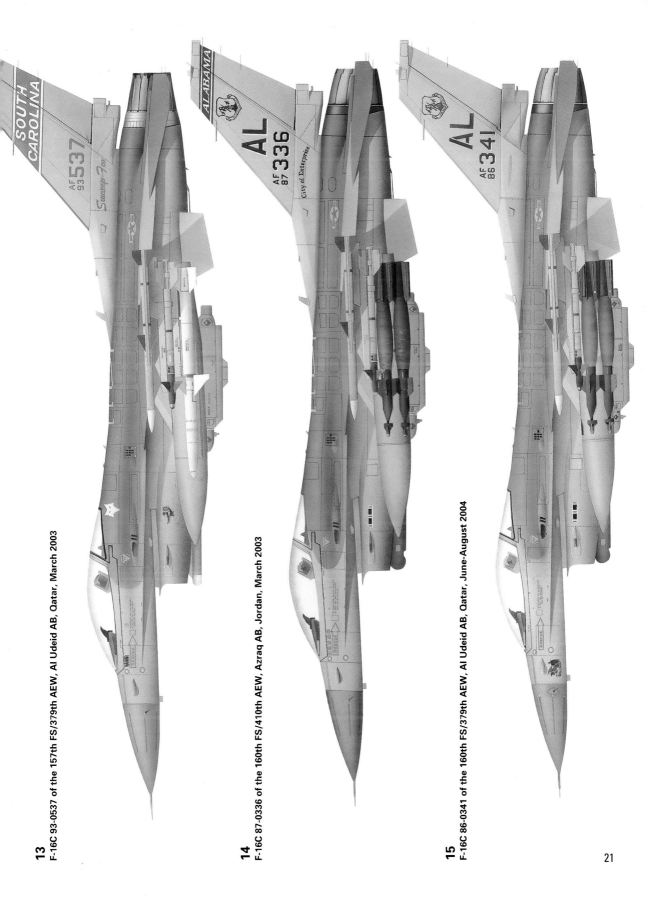

13
F-16C 93-0537 of the 157th FS/379th AEW, Al Udeid AB, Qatar, March 2003

14
F-16C 87-0336 of the 160th FS/410th AEW, Azraq AB, Jordan, March 2003

15
F-16C 86-0341 of the 160th FS/379th AEW, Al Udeid AB, Qatar, June-August 2004

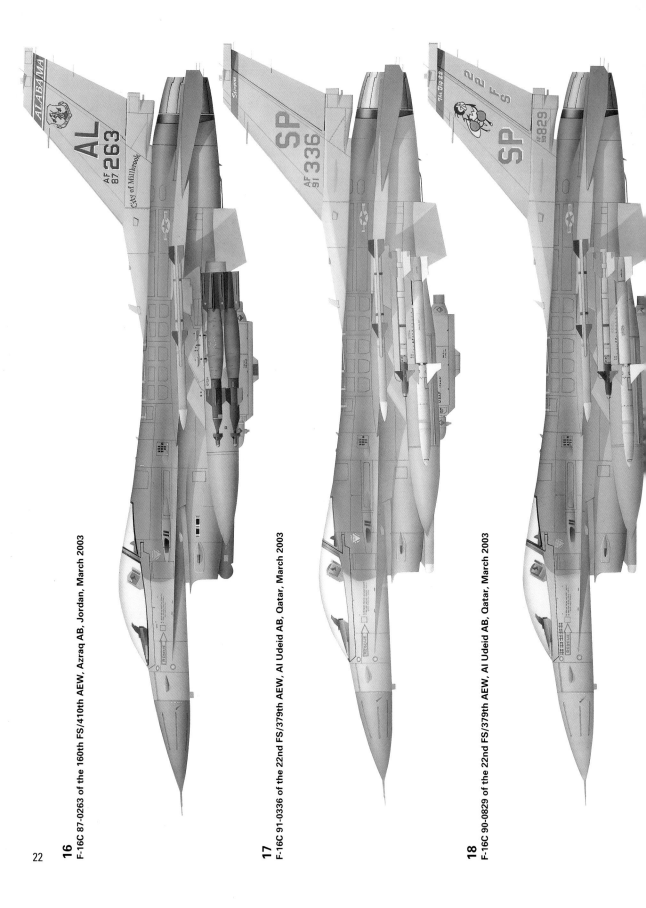

16
F-16C 87-0263 of the 160th FS/410th AEW, Azraq AB, Jordan, March 2003

17
F-16C 91-0336 of the 22nd FS/379th AEW, Al Udeid AB, Qatar, March 2003

18
F-16C 90-0829 of the 22nd FS/379th AEW, Al Udeid AB, Qatar, March 2003

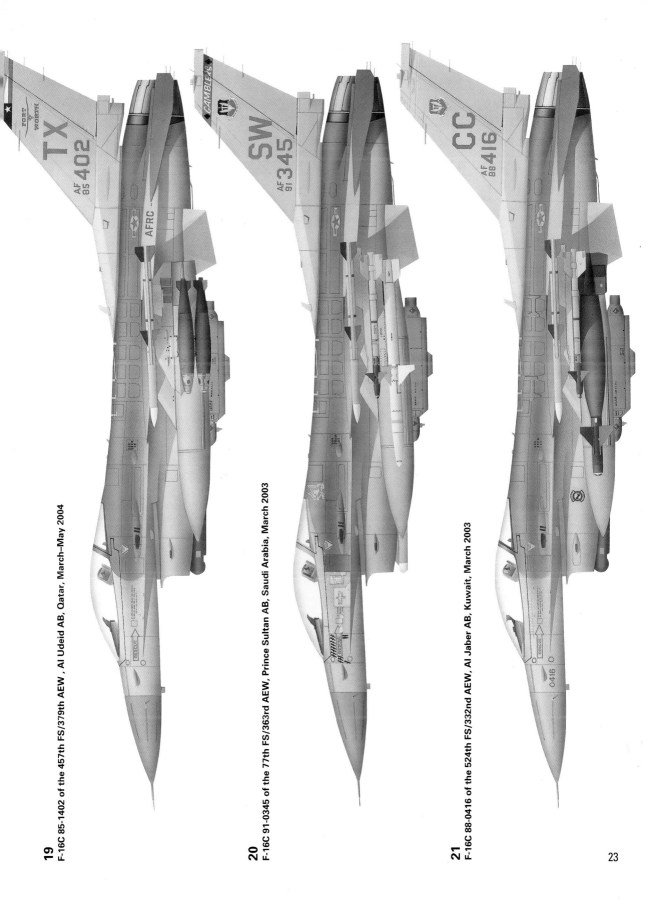

19
F-16C 85-1402 of the 457th FS/379th AEW , Al Udeid AB, Qatar, March–May 2004

20
F-16C 91-0345 of the 77th FS/363rd AEW, Prince Sultan AB, Saudi Arabia, March 2003

21
F-16C 88-0416 of the 524th FS/332nd AEW, Al Jaber AB, Kuwait, March 2003

23

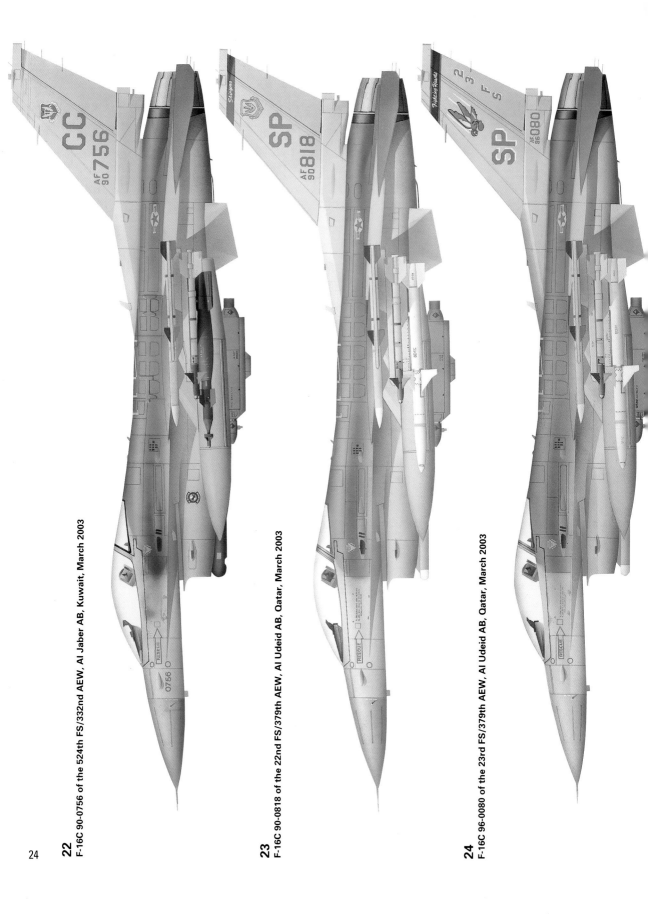

22
F-16C 90-0756 of the 524th FS/332nd AEW, Al Jaber AB, Kuwait, March 2003

23
F-16C 90-0818 of the 22nd FS/379th AEW, Al Udeid AB, Qatar, March 2003

24
F-16C 96-0080 of the 23rd FS/379th AEW, Al Udeid AB, Qatar, March 2003

77TH EFS/ 363RD AEW

'On 19/20 March we were flying on-call SEAD and had HARMs on board the aeroplane. I was a night guy, flying only at night, and it was early in the morning. I had one more vul to cover before I went home. We were covering six-hour vul times (vulnerability periods), where we'd come away to get gas when we needed it and then go back in again. I came out of the AOR (Area of Responsibility), contacted the appropriate agency, and they said, "Copy. You're going to support 'Ram 01'". That's all I got. Who's "Ram 01!?"'.

Capt Paul Carlton was a seasoned F-16 pilot with 1500+ hours of Block 30/50 time in his logbook. Only weeks before he had been plucked from the 55th FS at Shaw AFB to add NVG experience to the 77th EFS, and was leading a two-ship flight of F-16CJs on the last portion of their assigned vulnerability time when he had received this cryptic message.

'I had no idea what was going on. I asked, "Can you tell me who 'Ram 01' is, what their time-over-target (TOT) is and where they're going?" I got nothing back. Silence. The RoE was that we couldn't shoot or drop anything unless we were given permission to do so. That morning we were briefed that we were not to shoot any weapons unless were we told we could. So, I sent "Two" (Carlton's wingman) off to get permission to fire our weapons if needed, and at the same time I started looking for "Ram 01" on the radio. I had no idea what he was or what was going on.'

Completely in the dark, despite the impending tasking to support this enigmatic mission, Carlton was thinking that 'Ram 01' was probably a traditional asset – a Block 40 Viper, or some such. Little did he know that 'Ram 01' was actually an F-117 tasked with a time-critical mission to bomb a bunker in which Saddam Hussein was reportedly hiding.

The 8th EFS's F-117A 'Ram 01' came out of the night sky on 19/20 March 2003 without prior warning, forcing 77th EFS F-16CJ pilot Capt Paul Carlton to use all of his 1500 hours of Viper time to create an impromptu SEAD escort plan with only the most basic of mission information (*USAF*)

'"Ram 01" came up on the radio and told me roughly where he was and the coordinates of where he was going. He also gave me the coordinates of his IP (Initial Point) and his target, which I plugged into my jet so as to figure out where he was going and what his target was. His target plot fell into the little map of Baghdad. That clued me in to what he was about to do, and I knew that things were about to get much more exciting.

'Having learned the TOT and seen where he was going, I knew all I needed to know. I knew what threats he was up against, and now I was thinking about how best I could support him. I had just four HARMs to work with (two per F-16), which is not a whole lot to cover the entirety of Baghdad. Having devised a basic strategy, I flew back into the AOR, but chose not to go up near his target, even though we were now allowed to cross the No-Fly Zone. The F-16 is a radar-significant target, and I didn't want to stimulate the air defences before they needed to be. I never heard anything else from "Ram 01", which thinking about it now makes sense to me as the pilot always "cleans up" when they go to war (the F-117 retracts its communications antennas when entering hostile territory.'

Carlton continued to play it cool, but was still not aware of who it was he was supporting. He watched the SuperMEZ for about an hour, 'then I hit Bingo fuel. I had not seen anything happen to "Ram 01", so I told the controlling agency, "I'm Bingo and have to go home". I got handed off to different agencies and headed back to the tanker down south to get gas for the trip home.

'We were on the tanker when "Ram 01" came over the radio and said, '"Ram 01"', 'tanker 51', behind you and checking in for gas". As I came off the tanker with my wingman, I looked behind me and there's this "Stinkbug" taxiing up. That was the first clue that I had that we'd just helped start the war.'

'Ram 01' successfully struck the bunker, but Saddam Hussein would later appear on television alive and well. The mission was backed-up with scores of Tomahawk Land Attack Missile (TLAM) strikes, prompting Coalition pilots to watch silently from their cockpits as the cruise missiles made their way through the pre-briefed TLAM corridors to their targets, their heat signatures showing up on NVGs.

Only when 'Ram 01' reached the tanker on its outward leg did Capt Carlton fully realise that he had just helped make history. Saddam Hussein, it would later become clear, was still alive however. OIF had just begun (*USAF*)

The impromptu SEAD escort for 'Ram 01' came about 48 hours prior to the date that had originally been briefed for the beginning of the war. The subsequent 'Armageddon' that the public had been told to expect was never quite realised, and although 'Shock and Awe' may have been a little less shocking and not quite as awe-inspiring as many had thought it would be, Capt Carlton was more than happy with his performance on 19 March. Indeed, he had just performed a textbook demonstration of what he had spent nine years in the Air Force training to do.

'Most of our peacetime training centres on us learning rules-of-thumb and doing the calculations in flight so that when this kind of tasking comes during wartime, we don't need to do detailed planning there in the jet in order to get the mission done.'

OIF was now underway.

SEAD ESCORT

Meanwhile, at PSAB the squadron readied itself to fly its ATO-assigned missions. Foremost amongst these was the SEAD escort role, which saw each jet loaded with two HARMs and assigned to protect a Coalition package of 'strikers'. This mission required the F-16CJs to fly in close coordination with their charges on their way to the target, sniffing out radar nodes and specific threats and employing the AGM-88 from stand-off ranges in a bid to hinder the enemy's ability to shoot at the strikers.

A pre-planned mode available to the AGM-88 allows it to be fired at a suspected site regardless of whether it is emitting or not. Based on precise and thorough pre-flight planning, the timings are calculated so that the HARM will be in the air as the strikers are over the target, or at their most vulnerable point. If the threat radar comes on-line during the missile's time of flight, the HARM's seeker will detect the radar energy and issue corresponding guidance commands to steer it towards the source.

The main priority in OIF was to get threat emitters off-air as soon as possible, or to dissuade them from coming on-line at all. Early indications that the IADS would probably not operate cohesively, or with alacrity, would later prove to be more of a hindrance than a help.

For some 77th EFS pilots, OIF would be the most demanding experience yet of their short careers. Lt Eric Speer had received his Air Force commission in 1999, and had only recently graduated from F-16 training with the 162nd FS Ohio ANG prior to going to war. With less than 200 hours in the Viper when he arrived at the desert, he relied on 'dedicated and knowledgeable instructor pilots' to help him keep on top of the challenge. He performed well, and would end the war with a tally of eight AGM-88 shots, two Joint Direct Attack Munition (JDAM) and four Wind Corrected Munition Dispenser (WCMD) drops, in addition to 260 rounds of 20 mm ammunition expended. Lt Col Scott Manning explained the rationale behind deploying such inexperienced flyers;

'We did it the best way we could. The Air Force deploys units, and if your unit's combat ready, then why go and steal experienced guys from somewhere else? If this squadron gets the nod to deploy then this squadron's going to deploy. Twelve years ago they cherry-picked units and racked and stacked the deck, which I didn't necessarily agree with.

'Lt Speer was the youngest guy in the squadron, and Col Bob Beletic– the Operations Group commander – wrote a letter to the wing CO, Col

The F-16CJ carried the centrally-slung ALQ-131(V)-14 pod for self-protection for the duration of OIF (*FJPhotography.com*)

The size of the AGM-88 (right) becomes apparent when compared with the AIM-120 AMRAAM (left). This 77th EFS F-16CJ is seen undergoing last-minute checks on the ramp during the opening days of OIF (*USAF*)

Angelella, telling him that he should send Speer out to the desert. So he sent him.'

The 20th FW's previous OG, Col Tom Jones, had recently left the 'Gamblers' to take command of the 332nd AEW at Al Jaber, where he would end up flying combat in Block 40 F-16Cs. Angelella was a *Desert Storm* Viper veteran who, in early 2003, had to give up his role as 524th EFS commander at Al Jaber so as to assume his new position as wing commander at Shaw. As frustrating as this move on the eve of war from combat theatre to stateside operations must have been, Manning observed that Angelella handled it with good grace.

In keeping with their role to defend the battle space and other aircraft, the 77th and 14th EFSs were given the job of dealing with the SAM threat around Baghdad. The SuperMEZ comprised over 200 SAM systems, many of which were never pinpointed accurately by Intelligence, and it spilled over into the cities surrounding Baghdad. Whilst the 22nd and 23rd EFSs at Al Udeid would target the very heart of the MEZ, the 'Gamblers' and 'Samurais' would pick off elements of the SAM structure in the suburbs of Baghdad as Coalition strike requirements dictated.

Lt Col Manning flew his first OIF sortie on 22 March, and each member of his four-ship flight fired an AGM-88 against SA-2 sites located on Al Taqaddum airfield, to the northwest of Baghdad. His diary noted, 'I flew in support of some RAF Tornado GR 4 aircraft. We took some AAA fire and unguided missile launches, but nothing close'. Manning's next sortie saw him fly a similar mission to the Al Najaf area, although once again Iraqi resistance was light and uncoordinated. On 25 March Manning was tasked with providing on-call SEAD;

'After our second refuelling, we were tasked to depart the tanker and make a full-speed dash, without over-speeding our weapons, to Baghdad in support of a B-1B. I lit the afterburner and we raced 180 miles to Baghdad in less than 18 minutes. We arrived just in time to fire our HARM at known sites in the Baghdad area. The B-1 was bombing Saddam International Airport and some of its surrounding defences.'

That same day Capt Gene Sherer got to fly his first combat mission;

'I was SEAD mission commander, call-sign "Vouch 61", and we were flying in the SuperMEZ in the southwest corner of Baghdad. We were a four-ship supporting a B-1B, with some EA-6Bs doing jamming and some F-16CGs, F/A-18s and F-14s bombing targets. "Vouch 62" was Capt Matt Morrison, "Vouch 63" was Capt Jeremy Gordon and "Vouch 64" was Capt Brad Turner. We had one vul time that was supposed to be 25 minutes, but the CGs flexed late and Turner had a FCC (Fire Control Computer) fail, which was bad because it meant that he had lost most of his combat capability.

'Flying on-station, the next thing I know Dash-Four calls for a break turn. In the break I look and see a missile go straight past him, and I think, "Oh, shit!". We started to get a heartbeat going, and we were using the pod trying to do our stuff. Well, I ended up seeing another three missiles unguided, and at least two more that guide (optically) on me and my wingman, who was a mile-and-a half to the east in line abreast formation. All of it was unguided, but I later saw on my HARM tape that an SA-3 came online. I didn't see it at the time because we had AAA all over the place and my wingman was defensively manoeuvring. It was squirrelly, but the most incredible thing I've done. We all shot HARMs that day except poor old Capt Turner. We were in the MEZ for 45-50 minutes'.

On one of Lt Speer's first missions, he too narrowly avoided an optically-guided SAM;

'It passed about 200 ft off of my right wing. My flight lead (Capt Sherer) saw the missile first, and gave me a directive to break. There wasn't time to think about what had just happened. I just carried on with the mission, and with supporting the other aircraft out there.'

Capt Sherer and his wingmen received Distinguished Flying Crosses for their actions that day, and the former told the author, 'I'm still pissed to this day that I didn't get to shoot back at that SA-3 battery'.

Capt Carlton recalled that the on-call SEAD sorties would often result in them being tasked to strike specific SAM systems as they came on air;

'We'd get out our maps, work out where the target was and figure out the best way to go and hit it without getting shot at too badly. The horizontal situation display (HSD) in the F-16 is position-based, but its not so good at expanding different areas. We didn't know where all the SAMs were in the MEZ, so the best thing we had was the map that Intel gave us with the best information available to them on it. The best thing we could do was put an "x" on the map for our target coordinates and then look to see what known SAMs were around it. Then we could see what our best entry and exit strategy would be. We put that "x" on both our paper map and our HSD.'

The battle space across Iraq had been split up into 10nm x 10nm kill boxes to allow strikers assigned to CAS and interdiction to work specific areas and to provide deconfliction with other Coalition air assets, but the F-16CJs were allowed to roam wherever they wished during their on-call SEAD vul times. 'We weren't really CAS assets, and were only really TST assets in the sense that we had to go and hit SAM sites, but our primary job was to go and support the Army by making it safe for other aeroplanes to directly support the guys on the ground', Carlton explained.

Mission planning was accomplished by the Mission Planning Cell (MPC), which was a contingent of 390th FS F-16CJ pilots borrowed from the 366th FW at Mountain Home AFB, Idaho. The MPC took the ATO and broke it down, then planned and created briefing cards for the missions ahead. Having the MPC deal with the pre-flight administrative

The Horizontal Situation Display (HSD) screen is just visible on the pilot's right MFD from the rear cockpit of this F-16D. The HSD was a useful tool in OIF for plotting routes and maintaining situational awareness of known SAM threats (*FJPhotography.com*)

workload allowed the pilots actually flying the sorties to concentrate more on the fine details and the execution of the mission tasking.

ON-CALL DEAD

Within days of the war commencing, it had become apparent that the F-16CJs were going to find it more difficult to destroy Iraq's IADS than had been previously anticipated. The SEAD escort/on-call missions were proving to be successful insofar as the enemy was simply not radiating – whether by design, or because of their fear of the AGM-88 remains unclear – and the vast majority of those AAA fires and SAM launches that were being observed were unguided in nature. This unexpected turn of events, coupled with uncertainty as to the exact location of many of the known systems, meant that changes would have to be made. The solution was for the F-16CJs to re-roll into a DEAD mindset and assume a pro-active approach to tackling the problem. Maj Roberson explained;

'We'd planned pre-war that in a worst case scenario, based on the targets that we knew, and with evolving intelligence, it would take us 2.5 days with a 100 per cent success rate to exhaust the approved target list. Because of the factor of attrition, weapons effectiveness and so on, the worst case was that Day Five of the campaign would be the first time that we would actually start executing mixed loads on the F-16CJs – not everyone carrying HARMs – with some jets carrying JDAM, CBU-103 WCMD and CBU-107 that had been stored simply to take out those SAM sites where there was a high risk for collateral damage.

'However, the strategy that the Iraqis elected to follow meant that they did not come up and actively engage our aircraft, which presented a big challenge for us. So long as the threat is emitting, we have the sensor suite to detect it across a large frequency range, but because they chose not to emit and overtly target our aircraft, it made it very challenging to locate those threats. One can argue that because they chose to do that, that was suppression in and of itself. The very presence of the CJ meant we achieved SEAD. But that wasn't enough.

'We still had to execute an air campaign, so we needed to go "downtown" into Baghdad and "downtown" into Tikrit with LGBs and JDAM and hit some very important targets, and we had to get close to do that. So, we still had to sit down and work out what to do about the numerous threat systems that we had not located, and taken out, well beyond Day Five of OIF.'

For the 77th EFS, switching from the SEAD to DEAD mentality was a move that had been forecast before the war even began. Maj Roberson and those at the CAOC knew that Iraqi IADS resistance would not hold up for long, but no one had imagined that it would be practically non-existent. Those SAMs that did launch were usually guided optically, or fired ballistically for effect. As they got the measure of the threat, Shaw's SAM killers began to carry WCMD, as this jet clearly shows (*USAF*)

The solution came when 77th EFS CO Lt Col Jon Norman approached the CAOC and asked permission to start carrying mixed loads. Manning characterised Norman as a man who led from the front, who was one of the best tacticians he had ever met and who was adept at balancing risk management with an appreciation for the skill of his pilots. Norman, who made a point of flying a mission with his men every day, attended a meeting at the CAOC with Maj Roberson to hatch a plan;

'Gen Rew, who used to be the 20th FW commander, myself, the weapons officer from Misawa and Lt Col Norman sat in the Director's cab at the CAOC and talked. Rew had worked on developing a DEAD capability at the 20th FW when he was the wing CO, and he was now one of the CAOC directors. After the whole "superMEZ, don't know where they are, no one is emitting" discussion, Rew said, "Well, I know a wing that's been trained to do DEAD, and they're ready to do it".'

With a strong proponent of the 77th EFS taking the lead DEAD role, and with pre-war planning indicating that this mindset change would come within a week of D-Day, Roberson met with 'the weapons grads and tactical experts because we, the planners, weren't out there on "the point". So, we sat in the cab there at PSAB asking the guys if they can do DEAD, and they replied, "Yep". We asked them what munitions they needed and what timings were required?

'At that time we had a maximum of six jets swapping vul times going back and forth between the tanker. Ideally, they now wanted four of them to be available to deal with four-ship DEAD operations, so we now had to trade-off gas between them and the guys doing the CAS vul times. It was a zero sum game. So, we plussed-up the CJs and asked them to give us two more sorties per day. Two days later they started executing the new ATO.'

Lt Col Norman's unsolicited approach to the CAOC for permission to carry mixed loads had coincided with the realisation by Gen Moseley and his staff that such a change was both imminent and unavoidable. The F-16CJs would now proactively seek to score 'hard kills' against SAM and AAA systems using the medium altitude-capable CBU-103 WCMD cluster munition and the GPS-aided GBU-31 2000-lb JDAM. The CJs also carried the AGM-65 Maverick missile, which features an IR or electro-optical sensor to allow it to acquire and lock up the target visually.

Col Manning reflected that 'DEAD wasn't so much a coordinated mission against specific objectives, but more a case of "if you find it and can get permission to strike it, then go ahead and kill it"'.

On 26 March Manning and his wingman were once again tasked to fly on-call SEAD, but this time he was carrying two CBU-103 WCMD and his wingman had two AGM-88s. Arriving at the AOR, 'we received immediate tasking to drop CBU-103s on a SAM site south of Baghdad. There was an undercast, but the CBU-103 is fairly accurate and has its own inertial guidance system. When I released the bombs I watched them fall towards the white clouds below. The dark green contrast against the sunlit clouds was a picture that is hard to describe, but as they fell I knew that they were going to hit their targets, which would soon cease to exist. The fins on the bomb units deployed, and I watched as the canisters rotated and corrected themselves based on the winds over the target'.

Manning's flight had by this stage been joined by a HARM-toting two-ship of 'Gambler' CJs, led by Capt Sherer. He fired a single AGM-88 at the site to dissuade it from coming online, and three unguided SAMs penetrated the solid cloud layer but passed by harmlessly. Returning to the tanker for fuel, Manning was next tasked to support a B-1B striking targets in the middle of Baghdad. He instructed his wingman to fire both of his HARMs at known SAM sites in the area, leaving the vicinity once the 'Bone' had made good its escape.

FLEXIBLE TASKING

Despite the emphasis on IADS-related targets, there were instances where F-16CJs were reactively employed in much the same way as any Block 30/40 Viper. Capt Carlton was centre stage for one of the most inspirational stories to emerge from this type of mission when, on 25 March, he answered an emergency call on the Guard frequency for help. He and his wingman had taken-off from PSAB despite being told that there were no suitable landing fields in the whole of the theatre due to sandstorms and thunderstorms;

'We made our way to the tanker, passing through a thunderstorm that would come back into play at some point in the future. When we got to

Above and left
The 14th FS from Misawa AFB, Japan, added an additional punch to the SEAD capabilities of the 363rd AEW. Already in-theatre for OSW's AEF VII, the squadron was only too pleased to finally see some real action (*USAF*)

the tanker tracks there should have been about 25 to choose from, but there were only three or four that had made it out there in the weather. I found my tanker on the radar and then broke out of the weather about two miles in trail. As we got our gas, I looked north and there was a wall of cloud as far as the eye could see from west to east, going up to 36,000 ft.'

Heading north with his tanks topped-up with fuel, Carlton tried to take his wingman over the top of the thunderstorms, but soon got word from fighters coming out of Iraq that there was a break in the clouds between 15,000 ft and 20,000 ft.

'I took my wingman down and decided that I was going to try and dig up some SA-6s that we believed were in the Basra area – I would try and get him to shoot at me so that I could have some fun and shoot back at him in return. As we got up there, we were transitioning from dusk to night time, and I chose to go down through the thunderstorm. Well, I learned very quickly that the world goes from nice and clear, to light grey, to dark grey, to a mix of grey and red, then to black and then to green. After I saw the green I figured out that this was an electrical storm, and that I needed to get out of there!'

Carlton lit his afterburner and climbed back out of the storm, at which point the call on Guard came through. 'Anybody with JDAM contact me on this frequency', is what he heard. Carrying two 'cans' of WCMD, Carlton and another Shaw two-ship behind, also carrying two CBU-103, offered their assistance. The call had come from the US Army's 7th Cavalry, 3rd Battalion – the same regiment that Gen George Custer had so infamously led to slaughter at the Battle of The Little Big Horn in the late 1800s, and the same unit that was featured in the book *We Were Soldiers Once, and Young.* Located south of Al Najaf, the regiment had pushed north rapidly before bad weather had impeded further progress.

'The Iraqi Fedayeen are starting to suicide bomb them with cars and are shooting at them. They've got a couple of Ground FACs with them and they can't see more than 10-15 metres at best, and there are no air-to-ground guys nearby to help them out because they've gone', Carlton relayed to his wingman. They flew as fast as they could towards Al Najaf, but the entire region remained blanketed with solid cloud, preventing them from even glimpsing the ground. Meanwhile, the GFAC (call-sign 'Vance 47') organised his enlisted Tactical Air Control Party (TACP) members to map the perimeter of the friendly forces on the ground. With just a small measure of luck, and good timing, a 20-mile gap opened up between two thunderstorms straddling Al Najaf to the west and east.

'We got there and started talking to "Vance 47", and we worked out our coordination to drop. One of my WCMDs failed, and I didn't drop it because the problem was with the guidance system, but the other one went straight through the weather and hit the target. The lead pilot of the other two-ship also put his WCMD on target, and the feedback from the ground was very direct. They immediately came up on the radio and told us that they were no longer being shot at. This was great news, because when we'd been working out our coordination with him, we could hear bullets flying past his position as he'd held up the antenna for his radio!'

'We headed south, but I was already past Bingo fuel so we had to head for our divert base at Al Jaber, in Kuwait. I was calling for gas, but there were only three or four tankers airborne, when there should have been a

Top and above
The Wind Corrected Munitions Dispenser (WCMD) was used by Capt Carlton in support of the US Army's 7th Cavalry, 3rd Battalion on 25 March 2003. WCMD utilises a tail fin kit that can steer the weapon onto the target despite surface- and cross-winds that might otherwise cause it to drift. It is the CBU equivalent of JDAM (*Lockheed Martin*)

whole load of them. "Token 41" heard my calls and flew north to within five miles of the thunderstorm. He was a KC-10 – a huge aeroplane full of gas that doesn't mix well with thunderstorms – but he came and picked us up anyway. Sitting on the boom, I told the boomer what he and his crew had just enabled us to go and do. Well, the boomer must have got the guys up front to listen in, because as I left the boom I heard one of them say, "God bless you guys for what you're doing". I just turned around and told them, "this is what *you* guys made possible".'

The weather on 25 March had been so atrocious that it very nearly claimed a 77th EFS F-16 and its pilot, according to Capt Sherer;

'My Director of Operations, Lt Col Paul Schmidt, was in the weather when his Angle-of-Attack probes froze up and the jet went out of control. He had the choice of ejecting or staying with the aeroplane. He rode it out because if he had ejected, he probably wouldn't have survived. He ended up recovering control with just 250 ft showing on his altimeter.'

Capt Carlton was airborne when this incident occurred, and had heard Schmidt's wingman, 'Demon', screaming on the radios for Coalition fighters and Army Patriot missile batteries not to shoot at the lieutenant colonel's jet as it came screaming out of the clouds from 40,000 ft. Heading south from Baghdad, Schmidt was flying a profile that resembled an IrAF MiG-25 'Foxbat' on Coalition radar screens!

The weather improved marginally the next day, but when Sherer was asked to visually identify a convoy of 1000+ Medina Republican Guard vehicles heading south of Kabala, he was unable to get below 3000 ft:

'As soon as I hit the clouds at 15,000 ft I was about seven degrees nose down, and it was about as uncomfortable as I've ever been in an F-16. It was about 1600 hrs, so it was relatively bright, but I flew into a patch of cloud that firstly got dark and then turned dark red. At that point I got lit up by a threat radar and recovered about six nautical miles from the bad guys. The RWR started to go off, and I plugged in the "blower" (afterburner) and kicked out chaff as quickly as I could. It was worse than being shot at by missiles – that kicked ass – but this was not fun.'

The increased pace of these mixed-load sorties continued, with good degrees of success, and throughout the rest of March the 77th and 14th EFSs struck numerous SAM sites across Iraq. SA-2s were hit at Balad Southeast airfield as B-1Bs struck nearby cable repeaters and air defences, and SAM launch sites were investigated in the Kabala region as the Army and Marine Corps pressed on to take Saddam International Airport (on 3 April). An additional tasking emphasis at this time came in the form of Lane SEAD, which saw F-16CJs assigned to patrol ingress and egress lanes used by other Coalition fighters and bombers. Lane SEAD missions saw some of the most diverse weapons load-outs because seeking out targets of opportunity required absolute flexibility.

On one such mission in early April, Col Manning led a four-ship flight carrying two GBU-31s, four CBU-103 WCMD and two AGM-88s;

'We went north of Baghdad to an area between Balad Southeast and Samarra airfields, where we found a military compound with numerous SAM launchers and missiles. "Juice" and "2Dogs" dropped on the missiles with WCMD and then I did two passes with my JDAM and destroyed one of the sites. There were secondary explosions as the fuel propellant and other crap ignited from the explosion of my JDAM.'

Despite three of the four 'Gamblers' being 'Winchester' (out of weapons), one jet still toted its two AGM-88s, so the flight remained on-scene to escort some B-1Bs transiting the area en route to their targets.

The last exclusively SEAD missions flown by the 363rd AEW took place on 28 March, and 24 hours later Carlton earned a DFC. Scheduled to lead a night DEAD mission against two separate SA-2 sites, Carlton successfully struck each battery with a single WCMD whilst being protected by his wingman, who employed his AGM-88s against the sites pre-emptively. On 7 April Col Manning also earned a DFC during a particularly interesting sortie. He and his flight lead, Lt Col Dave Hampton, were scheduled to fly together in order to achieve their 1000-hour and 3000-hour F-16 flying time milestones, respectively.

Scott Manning had been an Air Force pilot for 16 years, flying the A-10 with USAFE prior to converting onto the F-16 in 1994. Despite all his hours in fast jets, he had missed out on ONW, OSW and all other combat operations. OIF was his baptism of fire, and he was relishing it.

Operating with call-signs 'Eli 21' and '22', the two F-16 pilots had originally been briefed to fly a Lane SEAD mission, but upon receiving fuel from their first tanker in atrocious weather, they were re-tasked by AWACS to perform a TST strike on Iraqi helicopters on the ground in northeast Baghdad. Marine Corps forces on the ground in the local vicinity complicated efforts to coordinate the strike, and just to make matters worse Manning and Hampton were loitering in a solid wall of cloud in the general area of Balad Southeast.

'This was at the time the regime was collapsing, and our tasking came straight from the CAOC through the AWACS. The weather was solid cloud from 37,000 ft down to 10,000 ft, and the airfield on which these helicopters was based boasted only a small 3000-ft runway. Where the information about the helicopter movement came from I don't know.'

Now well into the war, this 'Gamblers' jet boasts five AGM-88 silhouettes beneath its cockpit, each denoting a successful firing in combat. The orange sky behind the jets is an ominous warning that a sandstorm is not too far away (*USAF*)

And was the CAOC concerned that Saddam himself might be trying to escape? 'Well, the regime is falling, the Marines had pincered on the right side, the US Army had taken Baghdad International. Perhaps, then'.

Manning's jet was armed with a CBU-103 and an AGM-88 and Hampton's F-16 had two CBU-103s.

'There was some AAA fire and we had SAMs launched at us, but it was all unguided. We rolled in and I got one of the helicopters and Dan got the other two', Manning concluded. Both pilots had been targeted by an SA-2 and had been forced to manoeuvre aggressively to avoid the barrage AAA fire. With the TST tasking complete, they returned to the originally briefed Lane SEAD tasking in case Manning's AGM-88 was needed.

RIFLE!

Capt Carlton's final DEAD mission was typical of the mixed-load two-ship flights that had been flown in the weeks prior. It, like many of the later sorties conducted by the F-16CJs in OIF, was not exclusively anti-IADS in nature. Carlton's jet was armed with a pair of Maverick missiles whilst his wingman's F-16 carried two JDAM. He was leading his flight north of Baghdad when he called AWACS to ask for targets to bomb. Carlton was in turn given details of a Marine Corps FAC(A) team in an F/A-18D that had located ammunition storage bunkers.

'The storage area was large enough to feature on our maps, so we got checked-in, got AWACS permission to drop and the Marine guys gave us a centre point and told us, "You (Carlton) have the east side, you (wingman) have the west side". It was pretty much a fighter pilot's dream – they told us to pick anything we wanted to and didn't care what we hit, just so long as we hit something and then went on our way so as to make way for the next guys to come in and drop their ordnance.'

Coordinating with his wingman, Carlton discovered that his Dash-2 had never dropped JDAM before, and was unfamiliar with working the switchology for a visual delivery.'I restricted him and got coordinates from the FAC(A) to give to him. He went off and dropped on those coordinates. I then picked off two ammo bunkers with my Mavericks'.

The 77th EFS dropped several GBU-31s visually, and Capt Sherer also recalled that another useful delivery method for the bomb was the lob;

'You could lob that baby a *long* way. We'd get a call, "Hey, we want you to DEAD at this SA-2 site", and we'd simply type in the coordinates of the target, lob the bomb at the site and let the GPS take over and do its thing. That 2000-lb bomb was a real crowd pleaser.'

Although not usually associated with the F-16CJ community, the AGM-65 also proved to be useful in OIF not only because of its excellent weapons effects, but because it was the closest the 'Wild Weasel' Vipers came to using an electro-optical or IR sensor system to find and attack targets. Col Manning explained, 'We were hampered during OIF by not having a Litening II pod. All of our weapons – HARM, JDAM and CBU – have large explosive "footprints", so we were limited in the targets that we could strike. There were a couple of times when we checked in and were asked what we were carrying, only to be told that we couldn't be used, and that new targets were being found for us'.

The 'footprint' problem stemmed from the obligation placed on all Coalition aircraft commanders to conduct a PID (Positive Identification) and CDE (Collateral Damage Estimate) on all targets before rolling in and striking them. Doing so above the mandatory 10,000-ft minimum altitude hard deck was nigh on impossible with the unaided eyeball, and even with a targeting pod it was still challenging. Capt Sherer added;

'I'd have killed to have had a targeting pod back then so that I could have worked more effectively with FACs. A pod would have made life 150 per cent easier in OIF, and it would have allowed us to employ LGBs.'

According to Col Manning, 'The only other precision weapon we had was the 20 mm gun. We could strafe with that and roll in and be very precise. I never used the gun when our were troops in contact, but Lt Col Hampton did. He had a situation where he was called on to strafe a truck'.

When the threat required it – or when Coalition troops were in grave danger – the 10,000-ft hard deck limit could be disregarded, allowing use of the gun on several occasions. Manning did finally get to use the M61A1 cannon against an Armoured Personnel Carrier (APC) east of Samarra. Having expended CBU-103s on dug-in APCs and tanks, his only remaining ordnance was his PGU-28 20 mm ammunition. He flew back to the tanker for fuel, and was promptly informed by another flight of F-16s that there was an aircraft sitting on the runway at Balad Southeast airfield. He and 'Juice' strafed the unidentified IrAF aircraft, and on 'Juice's' second pass it erupted in flames.

By this stage of the conflict organised opposition was crumbling, and troops were capitulating across the theatre. The 'Gamblers'' original five-day SEAD tasking must have felt like a life time ago, as the squadron flew fewer and fewer anti-IADS sorties. Once Coalition forces had entered Baghdad, their role turned to enforcing the peace and attempting to quash occasional uprisings. 77th EFS pilot Donne Kang used a GBU-31 to drop a bridge in Tikrit during the last days of OIF, and on several occasions the unit performed 'shows of force', which were dramatic flights intended to quell those who might otherwise rebel against US and UK ground operations. Manning recalled one such flight on 11 April.

'The ground commander wanted to convince the local population of Al Hillah, south of Baghdad, that he could get air power any time he wanted simply by keying his microphone'. Of course, Manning and the ground commander had spoken before take-off to ensure the most dramatic effect, 'so here we come. I dropped down with "Chuckie" Middleton from 25,000 ft to 500 ft and hit the outskirts of the town. I was doing a mere 500 knots when I criss-crossed the centre of the town, lit the afterburner, stood the jet on its tail and went straight up. It was one of the best things I've ever done in an aeroplane. If you could only have seen the faces of the people in that town'.

Manning and Middleton left the area and went to work with a Navy F/A-18F FAC(A) that directed them to expend their Mavericks against tanks at Salum airfield. One of Manning's Mavericks came off the rail and nosed into the ground, but Middleton managed to blow the turret of his target straight up into the air following a direct hit.

FACTS AND FIGURES

Col Manning's 11 April mission was one of the final sorties in what is characterised as 'the shooting war' phase of OIF. From mid April there was sufficient authority on the ground to tighten the reins on ordnance

being dropped, and although the 'Gamblers' continued to provide reactionary and time-sensitive SEAD, DEAD and CAS services, it became routine to return home with ordnance still on the jet. Eventually the squadron was stood down from combat operations.

The 77th EFS had performed its duties with alacrity. Responsible for bedding down more than 300 personnel and 16 aircraft, Manning was later awarded the Bronze Star for 'his leadership, personal endeavour and devotion to duty'. In total, the 77th EFS employed 170 CBU-103s, 105 AGM-88s, 52 GBU-31s, 16 AGM-65s and in excess of 7000 rounds of 20 mm PGU-28. The unit had engaged 338 ground targets and destroyed or disabled 104 SAMs, radars and AAA pieces and 20 tanks/APCs, 26 trucks and 36 aircraft.

Under the stewardship of Manning, Capt Walters and Chief Master Sergeant Voigt, the maintainers and armourers from Shaw AFB had made it possible for the squadron's pilots to fly 676 sorties for a total of 3803.5 combat flying hours. All the while, the jets were maintained to a 75.3 per cent full mission capable rate.

An AGM-65D comes off the launch rail of a 79th FS jet and begins its journey towards some distant target during a live-fire exercise in the US pre-war (*USAF*)

Six Block 40 F-16Cs from the 4th FS/ 388th FW and six Block 30 F-16Cs from the 457th FS/301st FW, USAF Reserve, were also based at PSAB for the duration of the war. Here, a Hill AFB jet prepares to taxi away from the dispersal area, the aircraft carrying a 500-lb GBU-12 on Station 7. The aircraft has presumably been borrowed from the co-located, Reserve-manned, 466th FS for the 4th FS's OIF deployment (*USAF*)

379TH AEW

ike Lt Eric Speer, flying with the PSAB-based 77th EFS, several 52nd FW wingmen deploying to OIF were in their first operational F-16CJ tour. Some had been flying the jet for less than a year. Speer flew daytime sorties, but some aircrew assigned to fly the night shift at Al Udeid were equally as inexperienced as he was, and were not even NVG-qualified. Capt Ryan Peterson, who had just 150 hours in the Viper at that time, was one of them. Selected to fly a 22nd FS F-16CJ on the 8.3-hour direct flight from Germany to Qatar, he recalled,

'I qualified to fly with NVGs when we got down there. Some guys were to be day fliers, others night fliers, and a few would be both. I was lucky that there was enough time in the desert before the war started to complete the NVG upgrade programme.'

This was no small thing, as NVG 'guru' Capt Paul Carlton explained;

'The F-16 has had most of the NVG accidents, mainly because we have a different set-up in our cockpit. The main thing with NVGs is that we're not teaching pilots to do anything new or different. We're simply teaching guys to look through these 'toilet tubes' to get all of their SA (situational awareness), and then to integrate what they see with their instrument cross-check. With our primary mission being SEAD, we teach guys when firing the HARM to look away so as to avoid damaging the goggles, or to simply close their eyes. We want them to do both, preferably, so that the flash of the missile motor doesn't break the "gogs".'

Others like Lts Kenzie Jones and Tim Cole were not even afforded the luxury of acclimatisation, both pilots joining the 23rd EFS at Al Udeid on 15 March – a mere five days before OIF began. Cole added, 'We were in the last group to leave for Qatar, and we found out that we were going just 12 hours prior to our departure'.

The force protection mission is demanding enough at the best of times, but for these young aviators it would be a sapping experience. Not only would they have to maintain visual formation with their flight lead, they would also have to spend much time 'heads down' in the cockpit looking at the information from the HTS pod and the air-to-air radar.

Capt Peterson's first mission into Iraq was flown on 20 March, when his flight was assigned to provide SEAD support to strikers searching for mobile Scud missile launchers. Able to see strikes to the east being delivered by F-15Es, the mission proved uneventful until the time came to return to base.

'We were travelling along the Saudi border with 1900 lbs of gas,

Night Vision Goggles work by intensifying ambient light, but for all their advantages, they can also disorientate a complacent pilot (*USAF*)

looking for our tanker. They had made changes to the tanker tracks overnight, but it was obvious that they had also made changes to those changes! We couldn't see the tanker anywhere, and I didn't see anything on my radar. That was the most stressful part of the mission.'

The tanker track changes coincided with a complete change in the RoE – a necessary adjustment to accommodate the needs of full-scale war, but also one that has variously been described as 'stressful' and 'the biggest growing pain of all'. At a time when the younger Viper pilots were just becoming confident in their knowledge of OSW procedures, new 'Ocean Parkway' procedures governing the entry and exit of Iraq, refuelling tracks, reporting points and communications procedures also added to the strain under which inexperienced wingmen operated.

For Cole and Jones in particular, the pressure was on. 'My first flight, having arrived in-theatre on 15 March, took place on the 19th when I was sent to western Iraq', said Cole. Jones concurred, 'there was no in-theatre orientation flight or anything'.

Cole's first sortie, on the afternoon of 19 March, had lasted nine hours, and seen him complete five aerial refuellings. The roving force protection mission not only proved successful, but also ended on a humorous note;

'A funny thing happened as we were flying home along the southern border of Iraq. I got a SAM launch indication and did a defensive reaction, but the indication was for an SA-19, which is an IR- rather than radar-guided missile. This confused me at first because the SA-19 has a range-only radar, which is not detectable by RWR. By the time it went away I'd been "spun through the roof", and I was thinking that I'd been shot at on my very first combat sortie. When I landed and asked the crew chief about it, he replied, "Oh yeah, we've been getting that every now and again on this jet. It's just a malfunction". "Perfect", I thought!'

KILLING SAMs

Following on from the attempt to kill Saddam Hussein on 19 March, the F-117As continued to strike key objectives in the heart of the Baghdad SuperMEZ. On the second night of the war, Jones flew his first combat mission in support of an F-117 sent to strike a target in central Baghdad;

'It was my first ride in-country, and I had no idea. We had the Navy guys, who also wanted to go "downtown", on our assigned tanker and they wouldn't let us get gas. So, it's me, Capt "Scrub" Lane as my flight lead and "Amp" and "Yeager". We all had HARMs – eight in total – and we didn't know if the Iraqis were going to turn on their radars or not, so we were going to be firing pre-emptive shots. We only got about 2000 lbs of gas each, meaning that our external tanks were still dry and we had only our internal fuel to rely on. We turned off all our lights and pressed "downtown" in an offset container (box formation) in full afterburner. I was on NVGs, and all I could see were three big afterburner plumes racing "downtown".

'Flying at 30,000 ft and Mach 1.2, I wanted to know what the guys in the AWACS must have been thinking. It was full on. I was a little light on gas, so I kept creeping up on everyone else, trying to find the right afterburner setting to keep in position. We got to about two minutes from Baghdad and we knew that the F-117s should be just about to reach "downtown". In plain English, we worked our target sorting – "I'll take this one, you take that one" – and I was ready to shoot. I didn't want to shoot first, though, as I wasn't keen to be the one who screwed everything up! I waited for Dash-1 to shoot and then I took my shot.

'I was waiting and waiting and nothing happened. Then there was this *big* freakin' freight train of a missile whooshing right next to my canopy. You could smell the burnt powder of the rocket motor. What I didn't realise was that it wouldn't go high straight away. Instead, it was heading straight for Dash-1 and -2! I was scared stiff until the missile eventually climbed and did its thing.

'With four AGM-88s now airborne, we once again sorted out our targeting plan for our second missiles. We were still over the Mach, and there was all this stuff coming up from the city. I was thinking to myself "It's going to be the one that you don't see that gets you". My head was now literally looking everywhere in the sky and on the ground. In fact, I don't think I was actually looking at anything, because my head was moving so fast. We finally shot our second missiles, and then we realised we had used up a lot of gas. We were right over the SuperMEZ, and we turned around nice and slowly and went looking for a tanker.

'At this time the tankers were still over Saudi Arabia, but we eventually found a guy who flew into Iraq with all his lights on, blinking away. Everyone else in Iraq must also have seen him, and then Yeager overshot him! We asked if he'd make another turn north, and he told us that he would do it, but that it would be better for him if he headed *south*, as he was already over Iraq! "Scrub" and I hooked up with only 800 lbs of gas remaining – that's about five minutes' flying time, and we were still about an hour away from "The Deid". The four of us took it in turns taking fuel from the boom until we had enough to make it home.

During these early SEAD missions, the decision as to which specific systems should be struck first fell predominately to the flight lead, as Maj Roberson explained;

'If there were strategic SAMs out there that posed a threat, we let the guys flying the mission brief their own tactical game plan based on their own experiences. They held in reserve a targeting ability to combat those systems, and they then further prioritised the tactical systems based on targeting and salvo capabilities, acquisition and launch times, detection capability and range. So, at the operational level, we didn't say "shoot the SA-2 first". Now, we *would* say that an SA-5 (a system with a much greater range) would be prioritised at the operational level, because taking it out enabled most of the follow-on manoeuvres to be flown.'

The three F-16CJ squadrons at Al Udeid spent the first week flying force protection missions over western Iraq, but they also received a large number of SEAD escort assignments to protect specific packages striking targets in and around Baghdad. Protecting strikers did not always require the CJs be in visual formation with them, as pre-agreed timings could be used to make sure that both package and escort were in the right place at the right time. Knowing when the strikers would be operating in what areas allowed the Viper pilots to cue their HTS pods so that they were looking in the right areas, regardless of weather or visual acquisition.

'If the strikers were deviating from where they were supposed to be, the onus was on them to tell us. If they were out of position, or running a few minutes late, the important thing was for them to get that information to

us over the radio', explained Lt Jones, adding, 'Once we knew what they were doing, we could adjust our position to best affect our protection for them'.

For the first five days of OIF, HARM was usually employed pre-emptively, as SEAD pilots simply did not know what tactics the Iraqi SAM operators would be using, or which threat systems might come on air. One Viper pilot commented dryly that 'the Iraqis knew for sure that if they came on air they were going to get a face full of HARM'.

The AGM-88's most effective mode – and the one that the HTS is geared to provide data for which makes the F-16CJ unique among other US HARM shooters – is 'range known', where the missile has accurate azimuth and ranging information. This is the mode that offers the best probability of kill, and known emitter locations can be programmed into the missile's seeker head prior to flight, or passed dynamically via the ALICS during flight as the HTS 'sniffs the air' for electrons.

However, for much of OIF HARMs were launched using the pre-emptive mode, which allows the AGM-88 to be fired towards suspected or known sites in an arcing trajectory that maximises the weapon's time-of-flight. In this mode the missile seeker activates as it heads towards earth and then waits to see if its assigned target(s) comes on air. Lt Cole would fire two HARMs in this manner on his first sortie, and Lt Jones racked up a tally of eight pre-emptive AGM-88 launches – more than any other 23rd EFS pilot – within the first few days, leading to his temporary change of call-sign to 'Ocho' (Spanish for 'eight').

Top and above
The South Carolina ANG worked separately from the 22nd EFS in OIF, running its own MPC and being assigned its own target lines in the ATO. These photographs show the unit's HARM-toting F-16CJs at Al Udeid and over Iraqi in late March 2003 (*USAF*)

On those SEAD missions where a flight called 'Winchester', having shot off all of its AGM-88s, it could still continue to function effectively despite being out of its primary weapons. Maj Roberson explained;

'Just because they were "Winchester", doesn't mean that they'd return to base. The great thing about the CJ is that it is also a tactical threat warning platform. Because of its sensor capability, it can stand-off outside the threat rings and advise other aircraft of where the threats are. Plus, the enemy doesn't know if you've shot all of your weapons.'

Following the CAOC's decision that F-16CJs would carry mixed loads from the end of the first week of the conflict, the 379th AEW's trio of squadrons quickly re-roled to perform precision strike, employing JDAM and WCMD against pre-planned targets and TSTs, as well as in support of FAC(A)s and

Top and above
Loosing off an AGM-88 was something that always grabbed people's attention. The large rocket plume could be seen for miles around, and several pilots referred to the missile powering past the canopy as akin to a freight train passing close by! (*USAF*)

TAC(P)s in the CAS role. According to Roberson, these were roles that the Al Udeid Vipers were always expected to perform, but they were simply being asked to fly them sooner than was expected.

Most pilots flew once every second or third day, alternating between planning duties and ATO execution. Unlike some units in OIF, there was no surge of operations by the 379th AEW to cope with the faster-than-anticipated progress of the Army and Marine Corps on Baghdad, and it seems that pilots did not routinely fly more than one sortie per day.

The pre-planned targets for the F-16CJs flying from 'The Dirty Deid' were mostly fixed SAM and radar sites. On these missions, pairs of 'Wild Weasels' flew with mixed loads, where one jet carried HARMs and the other a mix of GPS weapons – typically one JDAM and one WCMD. Striking these sites in the first weeks of the war became routine, and the target list dwindled away until eventually there were none left. Roberson recalled, 'I sat in the CAOC watching the last threat system being targeted. There were no pre-planned missions after D+26'.

Accordingly, the emphasis on CAS and TST increased very early on in the war. CAS sorties usually saw a two-ship of F-16CJs assigned to support ground operations within a kill box, although there was no telling exactly what they would be called on to do once they arrived in-theatre. Sometimes, they struck hard targets such as ammunition bunkers, but additional targets came courtesy of other air assets. Lt Jones recounted the first time he dropped JDAM on one such sortie;

'There were a couple of F-15Es out to the east looking for their targets. We were a four-ship flight, and we told them that we had bombs. They passed us some coordinates that they would have used themselves, but they wanted to save their bombs for other things on this particular day. The other wingman and I (the two flight leads were equipped with HARM) put the coordinates for this truck, or embedded vehicle of some sort, into our system and drove straight to the target. We pickled our bombs off through the cloud, so I never saw what it was.

'Dropping JDAM was so easy even a monkey could do it. You put in your north, south, east and west coordinates, input your altitude and then drive to the target. The jet tells you when the bomb's in range and when it is at minimum range, and you can select the impact angle you want, and what route you want the bomb to take, if applicable. And that's about it.'

The 2000-lb GBU-31 derivative of JDAM was usually referred to as 'a crowd pleaser' that combined sheer destructive force with accurate targeting capabilities, but it was not always effective. When one 22nd EFS pilot was contacted by a SOF squad to drop on a guard tower being used by the Iraqis to spot Coalition troop movements, the JDAM struck at the base of the tower but buried itself into the soft soil below before detonating. The ensuing explosion may well have incapacitated, if not killed, the guards stationed atop the structure, but when the dust settled the tower remained standing.

Although different fusing settings could have been wired into the bomb on the ground prior to take-off, Lt Jones pointed out that standard impact fuses were used across the board, as they never knew what targets they would strike from one CAS mission to the next, and that this procedure offered the safest option for limiting collateral damage. Capt Matt Renbarger added that for pre-planned targets, 'sometimes the CAOC would tell you if you needed specific fusing, in which case they'd be set-up on the bombs before you took off'. In future, the planned introduction of the FMU-152 Joint Programmable Fuse will allow the pilot to set the fuse setting (delayed or air burst) in-cockpit according to the type of target to be struck.

Occasionally, only a show-of-force flyby was required to help troops on the ground. One notable example of the latter occured when soldiers were handing out water to a throng of parched Iraqi civilians. The crowd grew impatient and a riot threatened to ensue, so 22nd EFS F-16CJs flew low and fast over their heads to quell the unrest. Renbarger flew a similar sortie in support of SOF troops taking fire in northern Iraq;

'You could see the SOF guys easily – they had very recognisable black sports-utility vehicles (SUVs) that you could just tell were government vehicles. They were hanging out in a burnt-out courtyard, and we could see Iraqis coming at them from all four corners. All our guys wanted to do was get to a nearby bridge that would give them a better defensive position. We weren't ask to bomb because they were in the middle of a town, so we just came down to 5000 ft and let them know we were there. As we did that, we looked down and saw all the Iraqis doing 180-degree turns and hightailing it away as they heard the noise from our engines.

'I vividly remember watching this one white vehicle that heard us, slammed on his brakes and skidded into a ditch, with two guys jumping from it and running away. At the same time the SOF guys called that we had scared them off, and the four black SUVs just tore out of the courtyard and screamed out through the middle of the town.'

A single CAS 'line' in OIF would typically generate a tasking for six Spangdahlem or SCANG F-16CJs, allowing two to remain over the kill box whilst two cycled to the tanker and two others cycled to the kill box from the tanker. This cyclic process meant that at least two jets were on-station over the target area for the duration of the vul time.

Capt Peterson's most memorable mission was one such CAS sortie, when headed north on the wing of his squadron commander. The two Vipers were tasked with supporting an Army unit doing battle with an organised enemy force in a town south of Baghdad. As the HARM carrier, Peterson protected his flight lead as the latter dropped a JDAM and a WCMD on enemy soldiers that were using a football stadium as an elevated platform from which to fire upon the friendly forces;

'You could see those guys look up as the bombs came down. After the explosions, some of them tried to run away, so I rolled in to shoot them with the only weapon I had – the gun. We were at Bingo fuel though, so I pulled off after one ID pass and then we had to hit the tanker. By then the tanker guys were flying pretty far north, well over Iraq. They did it for hours on end, unable to see or react to threats, but they got no glamour or recognition. Well, they did a "kick-ass" job.'

On another occasion when an F-16CJ pilot used his 20 mm M61A1 Gatling gun to strafe a soft target on the ground, one of his PGU-28 rounds exploded prematurely and peppered the jet with shrapnel – it did not do any lasting damage, however. Incredibly, the pilot was not aware of what had happened until he landed!

Lt Jones also performed a night strafing against vehicles and trucks in the open. 'I never saw the rounds hit the ground, but on NVGs you can see this continuous stream of bullets fly out in front of the aircraft'.

Other CAS taskings saw some overlap with existing pre-planned targets, and one such sortie in particular stands out. Capt Renbarger was flying as a wingman, carrying a mixed load of JDAM and WCMD on a CAS mission, when he was called to strike two SAM sites;

'I was flying with Maj "Duke" Hornell, who I'd flown all of my missions with. We had sortied at night – we usually flew days – and were on the third of our four vuls when a USAF SOF guy on the ground called us up and gave us two sets of coordinates from his target book. One was for an SA-2 and the other for an SA-3 radar. We did our standard 9-line attack coordination brief which we always do for CAS. We confirmed our coordinates and I drove to the target, dropped the JDAM on the SA-2, turned 90 degrees to the right and about 90 seconds later put the WCMD pipper on the SA-3 site, hit the pickle button and dropped on him too.'

Renbarger had started his run in on his second target *before* his JDAM had even reached the ground.

'I never saw the JDAM go off because I was busy dropping on the SA-3, but I watched the WCMD hit and saw the perfect circle as it went off. It looked like fireworks. WCMD can provide more of a challenge to use if the target must be identified visually, as although you can do a 45-degree roll-in with it, it's not like a Mk 84, where wherever the pipper falls the bomb's going to go. You have to fly yourself to the right spot in the sky so that when the WCMD spins, it's going to do the right thing.'

The spinning motion of the CBU, and the height above the ground at which it dispenses its payload, determines the 'footprint' of the munitions as they fall to earth. Release the WCMD too low and the bomblets may fall in too tight a pattern to kill an area target. Conversely, if the canister opens too high, the bomblets may be spread too thinly, leaving the target still functioning.

TST taskings entailed providing cover for a series of preset vul times, ready to respond to an emerging threat that required immediate neutralisation. On the occasions where a vul period was complete and the F-16CJs were ready to return to base, they would usually advise AWACS of their remaining ordnance and subsequently be tasked to drop on secondary targets within particular kill boxes, or were directed to talk to FAC/FAC(A)s or ground commanders who wanted ordnance placed on specific targets.

Limitations imposed by the Viper's lack of a targeting pod became especially evident during the second week of OIF. The F-16CJ's inability to find and designate targets from altitudes that kept it away from lethal man-portable air defence systems MANPADS), which home in on the target's exhaust heat signature

Top and above
SCANG armourers prepare to unload a trolley of 2000-lb GBU-31 JDAM at Al Udeid (top), whilst (above) 22nd EFS armourers use a 'Hummer' to load a bomb onto one of their jets (*USAF*)

was a serious inconvenience. A mandatory hard deck limit of 10,000 ft over Baghdad and surrounding suburbs made it difficult for pilots to see aim points when FACs tried to talk them onto the target. Suffice it to say that F-16CJ pilots were dependent upon FAC(A)s and TAC(P)s for much of the war to find, (PID) and conduct CDE on their targets. Day time operations saw exceptions to the 10,000 ft rule, but for those who flew at night, the addition of a targeting pod would have been most welcome.

HIDDEN DANGERS

Despite the reduced IADS threat, and the incredibly low number of radar-guided SAMs reported by the F-16CJ community at large, there were at least two occasions where Spangdahlem jets were threatened in a serious way. 23rd EFS pilot Capt Renbarger, who was on his first operational tour in the F-16, was instrumental in the successful outcome of one of those occasions. Flying one of his first OIF missions, he recalled;

'"Duke" – my flight lead – and I were on our fourth vul, carrying two HARMs each that day. We were just south of Baghdad, and well into our eighth hour, heading south in line abreast formation going home when my flight lead was lit-up by an SA-2. Two guided SAMs were launched at

Top and above
Other than the obvious dangers of war, the weather was one of the Coalition's worst enemies during March and April 2003. Billowing sandstorms forced airfield closures, and towering cumulonimbus storm clouds that topped out at 40,000 ft had to be flown around – or through – to get to and from the target (*USAF*)

him, and he called the threat reaction and began defending against the missile – he rolled into the SA-2 and I did the same. As I looked down, I saw these two very large-looking bottle rockets corkscrewing from the ground with smoke trails behind, and they were pointing right at us!

'"Duke" had the full-up indications on all the RWR stuff we have telling him that these missiles were guiding on him. He was doing his defending, and I could see the missile site, based on where I saw the SAMs coming from on the ground. I point the HARM out there and took a quick shot at the site, before turning away and defending myself using the jet's EW gear. I rolled back and saw one of the missiles had blown-up about 3000 ft below me, but the other has disappeared.

'"Duke" then called for egress, and we turned south again, and as we did so, he told me that the second missile had passed over the top of him. The missiles were guiding, but we think that SAM operator shut-down as soon as I took my HARM shot.'

Renbarger had shown outstanding calmness under pressure, and his reactive HARM might just have helped his flight lead make it home.

A very similar incident occurred several days later when another young wingman heard his flight lead call that two missiles had been launched against him. Aggressively manoeuvring away from the weapons, he then reversed his turn toward the offending SA-3 site, acquired it with the HTS and unleashed an AGM-88. The site quickly went off air possibly because it had monitored the 'Magnum!' radio call that accompanies the firing of an AGM-88 missile, but more likely because this encounter occurred on a pitch-black night, and the huge rocket plume from the HARM gave a clear indication of what was headed their way. In either case, the SA-3s lost their command guidance.

Did the missile hit the radar site? 'I don't know' replied the F-16CJ pilot, 'but what matters is that the fire-control radar went off air'.

The F-16CJ's ability to react so swiftly to pop-up threats is almost entirely down to clever software programming and the hugely-successful integration of HOTAS (hands on throttle and stick) switchology in the cockpit. Capt Gene Sherer gave a step-by-step guide of how this works;

'The jet's smart enough that if we see something in the HTS pod, all we do is put our cursors over the threat and get a pretty accurate idea of its position, which will be good enough for us to launch a missile against it. At that point we designate the target and let the HARM go. We achieve the latter by moving the cursor switch on the throttle with our left thumb and use our right thumb on the designator management and target management switches – the DMS and TMS, which are on the stick. So, with the DMS forward to make the "hat" (HTS cursor) the sensor of interest and the TMS forward to designate the target, and hand off targeting information to the HARM, the pilot then hammers down on the pickle button to unleash the AGM-88.'

16th Weapons Squadron instructor pilot Capt Scott Ulmer, who was a 379th AEW OIF augmentee from Nellis AFB, was providing force protection for Navy F/A-18C and F-14 strike aircraft when bad weather forced him to fly well below his normal tactical altitude. Receiving intense AAA and SAM fire, he had successfully provided protection to the strike aircraft when his flight was re-tasked to destroy a SAM radar that was covering southeastern Baghdad. Still flying below the same inclement weather system, Ulmer was once again fired upon by AAA and SAMs before successfully neutralising the offending radar site. Egressing the area at full speed, he jettisoned his wing tanks to allow a faster escape.

Two days later, when flight lead for a DEAD force protection sortie, he once again came under intense SAM and AAA fire. Ulmer and his wingman made multiple passes at four separate targets (two SAM launcher sites and two optical guidance systems) to ensure their destruction – an objective they achieved with just four munitions. Ulmer was duly awarded the DFC for his actions during these two missions.

SAMs and AAA were not the only threat to life and limb in OIF. The insidious emotional rollercoaster that accompanied long hours in a confined cockpit, cycling to and from aerial tankers and in and out of hostile territory, gave grave cause for concern. So too did the threat from fatigue. 23rd EFS pilot Capt Jason Cochran gave one poignant example;

'We were primarily deployed in two-ship formations in a mixed element, one with HARMs and one with JDAMs. We had received a tasking and gone and dropped a JDAM and WCMD on a weapons storage facility southeast of Baghdad, and were waiting for a second tasking, when, ten minutes later, we had two SAMs shot at us. This incident took things to a new level, and made the sortie very personal. Looking like two bottle rockets, they definitely got our attention. We flew a defensive reaction and the missiles overshot. It gives you a high, and an emotional rush, and *that's* one of the biggest problems.

'Our typical sorties were six to nine hours long, with the longest being about twelve hours. During that time you could hit up to nine tankers for fuel. When the war started off, the tankers were in Saudi Arabia, so you had to come out of Iraq to get gas. Well, as you did that your emotions dropped, and you found yourself really dragging psychologically, and almost nodding off as you flew formation with the tanker.'

Nobody ever fell asleep in the jet as far as Cochran was aware, but the danger of it happening, with catastrophic consequences, loomed over their heads. Capt Renbarger agreed. On the sortie in which he protected his flight lead from the SA-2, 'we'd gone into Iraq and provided protection for guys twice already, so we'd spent a lot of time going to and from Saudi Arabia to meet the tanker. All the time we would be getting that "I'm in Saudi now, I'm safe" feeling, before having to get spun-up again to cross the fence back into Iraq'.

The incessant tempo of war makes it inevitable that fatigue will pervade a unit over time. Coupled with the physiological 'comedowns' that follow the body's production of adrenalin in stressful situations, the ensuing drowsiness and a loss of concentration could kill a pilot as sure as any SAM or AAA. Accordingly, the USAF looked to medicine for a solution in the form of the highly-contentious (at least to the media) amphetamine 'Go Pill', which 'worked like a champ' according to Cochran;

'My take-off times were primarily at night, about 0200 hrs (Local), and I would enter Iraq at sun-up. That presented some real challenges when you were trying to make the transition from night to day. The biggest thing with "Go Pills" was to keep taking them once you had started.'

The 23rd EFS's official squadron records from OIF reveal that there were 1773.6 combat hours flown across 268 sorties by the time the squadron returned home to Germany. This gives an average sortie duration of 6.6-hours. One of the longest sorties involved flying CAS for SOF operations being conducted in northern Iraq. One pilot recalled refuelling over Turkey, having flown all the way from Qatar;

'The tanker guy said, "Whoa! We haven't seen F-16s up here in a long time. We have a Combat Camera guy onboard – would you mind lining up here so we can take a picture?" So, there's this picture of a four-ship of F-16s (see page 50) lined up over Turkey. I had HARMs, my wingman had JDAM, Dash-3 had CBU-107s and Dash-4 had WCMDs. We had this great hunter-killer team that was ready to take on anything.'

23rd EFS chief mission planner Maj 'Bear' McAtee pointed out that these lengthy sorties also had an impact on the mission planning portion of the war;

'We'd get the order from the CAOC and they'd tell us who we were going to be flying with, and I'd take the whole package, coordinate with the different agencies and put together a plan for how we were going to work. We'd create products – maps and information – that the pilots could take into the cockpit with them. The pilots came in, briefed the

mission quickly and then went flying. The missions were so long that they didn't have time to do the mission planning. Our goal was to create a set of instructions that a guy could walk in "cold turkey", know what he was going to do and go out there and do it.'

McAtee himself alternated between flying missions and heading the mission planning cell (MPC).

ANOMALIES

On 25 March Maj Douglas Blouser was leading a flight to Baghdad when an Army PAC-3 Patriot missile battery targeted him. Reacting instinctively, the 23rd EFS Weapons Officer unleashed a single AGM-88 in self-defence, resulting in damage to the Patriot's radar. The incident occurred about 30 miles south of An Najaf, and just 24 hours after an RAF Tornado GR 4 was downed by a US Patriot with the loss of both crew. Blouser's actions preceded a second Patriot friendly fire incident on 2 April, when a US Navy F/A-18C from VFA-195 was shot down and its pilot killed (see *Osprey Combat Aircraft 46* for details).

For the tactical aviators in-theatre, the Patriot was already a major concern by the time that the RAF Tornado was lost. In order to ensure that it did not fire at a Coalition aircraft, pilots had been advised to use not only their military, encrypted, Mode 4 identification friend or foe (IFF) transponders, but to also activate their civilian Mode 2 IFF as well. Although this made them less likely to be targeted by the Patriot, it also provided some of Iraq's SAM systems with a means of tracking their movements. In a worst-case scenario, some Iraqi SAMs could even use Mode 2 IFF transmissions as a source onto which they would home!

It is clear from on- and off-the-record conversations with individuals from several communities that the Patriot posed a greater concern to them than anything in Iraq's arsenal.

But what of the cause of these shoot down incidents and Blouser's fratricide against the Patriot? There seem to be two common observations. The first is that the RoE allowed the fratricides to occur. 77th EFS DO Lt Col Manning had this to say;

Cycling to and from the tanker presented perils of its own, as multiple trips to the boom, fighting spatial disorientation and refuelling in weather that peacetime rules would have kept everyone grounded were all the norm over Iraq (*USAF*)

'I think that the responsibility for the weapon's use rests squarely with the Army. The whole thing about losing a British jet and a Hornet to the Patriot is the RoE that goes into it. When is the Army allowed to put the system into automatic mode? When can they pull the trigger? If the RoE is stringent then you don't have a problem, but if it's too free or loose then you open up the door for decisions to be made that have tragic consequences.'

The second observation commonly made is that the standard of communication between the Army and the Air Force was lacking. Indeed, it was this latter failure that led directly to Blouser's HARM shot in self defence. The 23rd EFS's Maj McAtee concurred;

'It seemed like everything was happening so fast – which was good in the sense that we were moving forward – but the Army was not coordinating with us to tell us where they were, who they were and what was going on. In my opinion, we didn't have a good enough picture of what the Army had. And it's not just what's located on the ground – it's what emitters do they have, what radars and what electrons are they throwing out into the air? Our aeroplane is mechanised to sense all of these things and adapt accordingly. We have to know what both the good guys and the bad guys are throwing out electronically so that we can distinguish between them. If we don't know, we can't programme the software to do that.'

McAtee may well be alluding to the fact that the F-16CJ's HTS was not programmed to 'recognise' the signature of the Patriot's radar, forcing the RWR to display it as an 'unknown' SAM, and thus confuse matters still further.

Col Manning was in no doubt that the F-16CJ squadrons in OIF were in desperate need of Army ground liaison officers (GLO);

'Having a GLO available to us would have put us more at ease because we'd have had the ground order of battle. Now, some of us who have experience in other platforms – like my time in the A-10 – were constantly telling the young guys, "Find out where the Army is". So, we were getting our Air Force Intel guys to tell us where the Army and Marine Corps guys were. It doesn't take a brain surgeon to work out that once you know where the main Army formations are, there are going to be air defence assets around them'. And Maj McAtee makes no apologies for what happened with the HARM Patriot shot. 'We had no idea where the Patriots were, and those guys were locking us up on a regular basis. No one was hurt when the Patriot was hit, thank God, but from our perspective they're now down one radar. That's one radar that they can't target us with anymore!'

Interestingly, the F-16C was the only platform during OIF to carry the CBU-107, or Passive Attack Weapon, which behaves like a WCMD but contains no exploding sub-munitions. Instead, it is packed with steel rods that are meant to puncture TBMs suspected of containing WMD. An Al Udeid pilot explained to the authors precisely how this weapon worked;

'If you blow the Scud up you have a big cloud of chemicals that might end up killing civilians – this weapon will use different size steel rods to puncture the SCUD or penetrate a storage dump's roof so that they don't blow up, but are no longer fit for use. Pilots were under strict instructions to employ it only against TBMs, and it was never used apart from the one release when a McEntire (SCANG) guy expended one against a target he shouldn't have!'

There were other anomalies that stand out from the 379th AEW's deployment. At one stage the Army decided to utilise its AH-64 attack helicopters in the deep strike role, simultaneously tasking the F-16CJs at Al Udeid to support them. The reaction in Qatar was one of incredulity that the Army had failed to appreciate that deep strike was a role in which the F-16CJ was perfectly capable itself, and that it would unnecessarily put its own helicopter crews in grave jeopardy. When the AH-64s failed in their efforts to undertake this mission, it took all the will power in the world for the Spangdahlem crews not to turn to the Army and say, 'I told you so'. Of course, the Air Force learned lessons, too.

One major gripe that became evident whilst researching this book was that there were significant lapses in the efficiency of the command and control structure. Time and time again pilots would recall that some of the most harrowing memories of OIF come from the inability to find a tanker at the end of a mission when fuel was critically low.

'We'd call for our tanker, ask AWACS where he was and be told, "He's gone home already". "Well, no one's told me", I'd reply', said one F-16CJ pilot. This poor coordination also extended to the battlefield. 'We'd take off without a target, fly for eight hours trying to get someone on the ground to give us something to drop on, and then we'd come home with our bombs on board. It was frustrating for guys who wanted to feel like they'd contributed to the mission', Maj McAtee recalled.

In response to the gripes emanating from Al Udeid, McAtee recalled, 'my good friend Maj Mark Cline, who had planned much of the war, sent us an email saying "Okay, I hear you guys. We're going to start Operation *Home Depot*, and we're going to go out into the desert and build you some targets so you can drop your bombs!" That made us laugh, but what he was really saying to us was that we had still done our jobs, even if we came home with all our bombs'.

Typical of the effort made by the 379th AEW's trio of Viper units, the 23rd EFS had flown 268 sorties, for 1773.6-hours, fired 53 AGM-88s, dropped 47 GBU-31s and 28 WCMDs and shot 779 rounds of PGU-28 during OIF.

524TH EFS/ 332ND AEW

The 524th FS 'Hounds from Heaven' have historically been a component of the 27th FW, which has been stationed at Cannon AFB, New Mexico, since 18 February 1959. For most of the Cold War the 'Hounds' flew the General Dynamics F-111D/F strike fighter, converting to the F-16C Block 40 Viper in July 1996.

The unit had been to 'the sandbox' for OSW twice before – once in the late 1990s, when it flew for 45 days out of PSAB as a part of the 4404th Wing (Provisional), and then from Al Jaber as part of 332nd AEW in September-November 2000. The squadron dropped bombs in anger for the first time with its new F-16CGs during the course of the latter deployment, expending 23 GBU-12s and knocking out two air defence radar sites, a Roland SAM and some S-60 AAA guns.

Lt Col Tom Berghoff took command of the unit in July 2001 and led the 'Hounds' (15 F-16CGs and 352 personnel) to Al Jaber as part of AEF VII in December 2002. At the time of this deployment, tensions were escalating, and there was already a mounting probability of open warfare. Berghoff prepared his squadron accordingly;

'We did a lot of prep before we even left for AEF VII, my senior pilots and I looking at what we thought would happen if a war did kick off. There was a lot of rhetoric going on, so we assumed that while we were down there it was going to happen. We looked at the most probable scenarios, and the types of missions that we would primarily be tasked to perform, and cleaned up before we were deployed. We highlighted those types of missions in the flying programme, and we were pretty much spot-on when it came to our training focus, and the types of missions that we would eventually be tasked to fly in OIF.'

Deploying to Kuwait – and therefore very close to the battlefield in the event of either another Iraqi invasion, or a Coalition ground offensive – the 'Hounds' were charged with providing CAS for friendly ground forces. While the co-located A-10A Thunderbolt IIs would provide the very close-in air support at the front with their 30 mm GAU-8/A Gatling gun and Maverick IR and electro-optically guided missiles, the 524th trained to use its LGBs and JDAM to destroy specific high value targets – concentrations of armour, supply dumps, headquarters, communication nodes, etc. – just behind enemy lines. Also at Al Jaber were Marine Corps AV-8B Harrier IIs and F/A-18C/D Hornets, which provided the same close-in and behind the lines air support for the Marine Corps in contact.

All pilots in the squadron immersed themselves in training in preparation for war, especially the the newest lieutenants. One of the latter was Lt Chad Martin, who arrived at Cannon in June 2002 and completed Mission Qualification Training (MQT) on 1 August. The

youngest 'Hound' initially selected to participate in the AEF deployment, he stated that the main training leading up to the deployment was by providing Weapon Instructor Course (WIC) support – flying as strikers on the Nellis Ranges for WIC students (future Weapons Officers) so that they could practise intercepting. Additionally, there was a focus on employing LGBs and JDAM in the CAS and deep strike roles;

'We also had a trip to Exercise *Air Warrior II*, held at Barksdale AFB, Louisiana, where we focused on CAS using LGBs and JDAM. Training at home leading up to the deployment centred on LGB and JDAM employment as part of a strike package, but not so much in the CAS role. There was almost zero emphasis on air-to-air.'

The 'Hounds' became most proficient at using the AAQ-14 LANTIRN targeting pod, affixed to the right cheek of the jet's 'big mouth' air intake, when it came to guiding their GBU-10 (2000-lb) and GBU-12 (500-lb) LGBs onto the target. The navigation pod, formerly mounted beneath the left intake cheek, had been removed some years earlier when Viper tactics changed from night low-level ingress/egress to medium altitude approaches cloaked by centreline-mounted ECM pods

The first 12 Vipers of the 524th FS 'Hounds' arrived at Al Jaber AB, Kuwait, on 18 December 2002, carrying their fuselage-mounted AAQ-14 LANTIRN and AN/ALQ-131 ECM pods and a triple ejector rack (TER) under each wing. Hung from the bottom lugs of the TERs were MXU-648 Travel Pods, filled with the pilot's luggage and extra equipment (*USAF*)

Al Jaber was 'CAS Central' in OIF, the 'Hounds'' 20 F-16CGs being augmented by 50 Fairchild A-10A Thunderbolt IIs to make up the 332nd AEW. Co-located at the Kuwaiti air base were a squadron of Marine Corps AV-8B Harrier IIs, five squadrons of F/A-18 Hornets and two squadrons of RAF Harrier GR 7s (*Capt Ed Bahret*)

and the abundant jamming assets in the USAF and US Navy/Marine Corps electronic battle array.

Many – especially F-15E Strike Eagle aircrew – have doubted the ability of one person to both fly the jet and employ the laser guidance system for targeting, but such concerns were dismissed by high-time Viper 'driver' Lt Col David Kossler;

'The F-16 was designed for one person operation, being easy to fly. Granted, much of your attention when you're in the target area is in doing your target area work, but it's not all encompassing as long as you do a good target study and thorough mission planning. There are ways to point the targeting pod that ease the mission load, for example. You can look at the ground through the HUD and stabilise the pod on a spot that you see, and it keeps track of it. So now it doesn't matter what you do, as the targeting pod will always be pointing at whatever you look at through the HUD.'

Kossler, who has 3000 F-16 hours to his credit, was the 524th FS's Assistant Operations Officer (ADO) for the OSW/OIF deployment. He feels the ability to designate targets through the HUD 'is actually an advantage in a single-seat jet, because if you see a target nearby – like tanks for instance – you can just stay in a "wheel" (orbit over the target area) and roll in, designate, put the pod on it, hammer down and the pod stays there to illuminate the target for the time of flight of the bomb. The Strike Eagle normally makes straight runs at the target. In the Viper community we normally just hang out in a "wheel" over the target area and just keep rolling in and dropping our bombs when we see something to hit.'

Once the training was 'cleaned up' and the unit ready for deployment, the 524th departed in mid-December for 'The Jab'. While the planning and preparation were complete, the movement was still subject to the vagaries of nature and mechanical bad luck. The first 12 F-16CGs departed Cannon on time and made the first leg to Moron, but the En route Support Team Aircraft (a Lockheed C-141 Starlifter) had some difficulties. It was forced to land at Gander, in Newfoundland, Canada, and was stuck there for five days in a blizzard. Once it arrived at Moron, it broke! After another five-day delay, Lt Martin related, 'We finally rolled in to Kuwait International Airport at about 0430 hrs on Christmas morning. We had to unload our own aeroplane, and showed up at Al Jaber at about 0830 hrs.'

But finally the 'Hounds' were all in place, patrolling southern Iraq enforcing the No-Fly Zone, ready to perform on-call Response Option (RO) strikes should Iraqi IADS become active and sitting 'Apollo Alert' to guard against the IrAF using the twice-daily Baghdad to Basra Shuttle (an Iraqi Airlines Airbus A320) to mask the movement of its fighters south into the NFZ by hiding in the Airbus' substantial radar signature.

Being based so close to their AOR had distinct advantages. As Lt Col Berghoff said, 'being there for AEF VII and flying around in the airspace helped a lot. We didn't go "downtown" into Baghdad and its SuperMEZ pre-war, but we were at least familiar with the local flying in and out of southern Iraq , and that proved crucial for us when it came to dealing with the CAOC's procedures for OIF.'

The squadron expended 176,500 lbs of munitions in RO strikes during OSW, setting a record for ordnance dropped by any USAF unit in

The 524th EFS was commanded by Lt Col Tom Berghoff, who had previously flown Vipers at Kunsan AB, Korea, and Ramstein AB, Germany, and had also been an instructor at Luke AFB, Arizona. He took command of the 524th in July 2001 after serving on the NATO CAOC during Operation *Allied Force*. (*Unofficial Squadron Yearbook*)

AEF operations. These were mainly some 87 2000-lb JDAM which the squadron, taking advantage of Iraqi threat reactions as an excuse to prosecute the OIF 'battlefield preparation' phase, employed against Iraqi cable repeater sites, thus dismembering the enemy's communications network. Additionally, five GBU-12s were used against air defence assets.

These strikes also provided the 'Hounds' – including the youngest one present – with much-needed combat experience against other types of targets. As Martin related, 'I had flown eight or so "Strike Fams" (familiarisation sorties) into southern Iraq, but had no expenditures until 11 February. While sitting "Apollo 3/4" (ground alert for RO strikes), we were informed that Intelligence had found some Al Samoud missiles near Basra that they feared had chemical tips. We waited most of the day for SecDef (Secretary of Defense) Rumsfield to approve the target, and finally as night fell we launched a four-ship loaded with two JDAM each.

Leading the mission was squadron CO, Lt Col Berghoff, with Lt Steve Engberg on his wing. Martin's flight lead was Capt Bryce Hardy;

'Berghoff and Hardy had instantaneous fuses to destroy the launchers and Engberg and I had airburst fuses (20-ft burst altitude) to hopefully kill any chemicals that the missiles might contain.

'We were cleared to enter Iraq and drop before we took off, so when we got airborne we just went high and fast and drove in to Iraq in an offset container ("box" formation). When we initially pushed in-country we made it look like we were flying one of our normal strike fam routes that we would take on a nightly basis, but then, all of a sudden, we turned south towards Basra. Once we were all within parameters, we just started dropping. We all dropped both of our bombs on one pass – Berghoff and Hardy took out the TELs (Transporter-Erector-Launcher vehicles), and Engberg and I took out the missiles. Awesome secondaries! It was my first live drop, and then we "got out of Dodge!"

'I think we were almost back across the line before they really knew what had happened. We did see some AAA, and the first time I realised I was actually being shot at was when we had AAA going off around us.'

As the unit's designated AEF period approached its end, the 524th looked like it might rotate home on time. But the squadron commander was told otherwise;

'We were due to rotate out in March. We were held in place and then obviously OIF kicked off just about the time that we were supposed to head back home. So we stayed there throughout, and we re-deployed home on 12 May after the air war wound down.'

THE 'HOUNDS' GO TO WAR

'Well it started! Today was D-Day for the war. I flew and dropped one of the first bombs of the campaign'. Thus reads the first entry of the OIF chapter in Lt Russ Piggott's journal,

'Norris 25', which was the first OIF mission to be performed by the 524th, was flown by (from left to right) Lt Col Rob Givens (Ops Officer), Lt Steve Engberg, Maj Wade Dewey and Lt Russ Piggott. Their take-off time was 1925 hrs, but because 'Hound' tradition states that for a lieutenant, everything must end with '24', Piggott logged his departure time as 1924 hrs, thus officially becoming the first 524th EFS pilot to take off on an OIF sortie! (*Russ Piggott via Author*)

kept during his 158 days at Al Jaber. This first night he was 'Norris 28', or Dash-4 on the wing of 524th FS DO, Lt Col Robert Givens;

'Our mission was to destroy communication sites – a series of small buildings that housed fibre optic switching equipment – 50 miles west of the Iraqi capital. It was a great night to fly, the moon was just past full but there was a low-level haze from the dust. We were "Norris 25", a flight of four F-16CG strikers. I took off at 1924 hrs, joined up and headed west.

'New procedures were in effect for air-to-air refuelling, and we were allowed to go into Saudi Arabia – something we were previously restricted from doing due to political reasons. We hit the KC-135 and topped off with plenty of fuel for the rest of our mission north. The F-16CJs joined us on the tanker and pushed out just in front in order to get to their CAP point to support our strike. It was 200 miles from the tanker to the target area – a long way over Iraq on the first night of the war.

'As Dash-4, it was my job as a wingman to clear my flight for threats, and that's what I was doing on the way up to the target area. There was nothing coming towards us. About 40 miles to the north was Al Asad air base, housing MiG-25 "Foxbats" capable of chasing us down at Mach 2.8. I was expecting the IrAF to scramble those guys because we were above the 33rd parallel – unfortunately they didn't.

'We pressed to the target, which was just along the highway to Jordan. Givens was hitting a building just behind a rest stop with BLU-109 JDAM penetrators. There was a mosque about 500 ft away, but the CDE was okay due to the fuse delay on the bomb. Maj Wade Dewey hit another building about half-a-mile away to the north, and my building was about 1000 yards away from his. We dropped our bombs on time for a 2106 hrs TOT (Time Over Target), then turned to the south, away from the threat. There were no threats seen during the entire flight, and it was pretty uneventful.

There was a worse haze layer when we returned, and I had to shoot an approach down to minimums. It was really exciting to be out on the first night of the war, dropping some of the first bombs.'

Back at Al Jaber the 'Hounds' – aircrew and groundcrew alike – fully realised they were at war when the Scud alarms sounded and everyone was ordered into their MOPP 4 (Measure of Personal Protection level 4 – the full chemical warfare ensemble) gear. SrA Cynthia Schlegel, who was one of the dedicated operations clerks, reported that for the 'Hounds' on the

While being close to the front greatly facilitated the 'Hounds'' ability to support the ground forces, it also meant that the unit was within range of Saddam Hussein's remaining Scud missiles. During the first week of OIF, Scud Alerts occurred frequently, forcing the groundcrews to launch their Vipers while dressed in MOPP 4 – the full chemical defence ensemble (*Unofficial Squadron Yearbook*)

The 524th EFS's intelligence section poses in MOPP 4 inside the unit's Ops Building. According to SSgt Heather Kraft (far left), the television in the upper left corner of photograph was the primary warning source for Scud launches. Typically, three minutes before the official warning arrived from the CAOC at PSAB, Fox News reporters would announce the Kuwaiti Scud alert. She said, 'When we saw the Fox News reporter put on his helmet and gas mask, we knew we had incoming!' (*Unofficial Squadron Yearbook*)

The Mk 129 leaflet bombs were originally designed as CBU dispensers. Triggered by an airburst FMU-14 fuse, the containers, packed with paper leaflets, would split open at a preset altitude, showering the messages upon the enemy. The 'Hounds' dropped 31 Mk 129s prior to OIF beginning, and another 108 during the offensive itself (*USAF*)

ground, the first indication that OIF had begun was when the Kuwaiti 'Alarm Red' was sounded while watching CNN from the ops desk. 'I was sitting at the desk with Lt Col Berghoff, and we were watching CNN when the Kuwaiti alarm went off first on TV, followed by the base alarm. That was my first real clue that it was starting.'

SrA Schlegel, working 12-hour shifts and barracked on base, was subject to all the Iraqi counter-attacks aimed at their small host nation. The 'Alarm Reds' sounded any time of day 'four to five times a day at first, for the first week. And then it went down to maybe two times a day. It would happen in the morning or the evening. There was no set pattern'.

Sometimes the alarms would catch pilots on the ground between sorties, as the 524th FS's Lt Russ Piggott reported;

'After my first mission I was rudely awakened at 0920 hrs the next morning by the "Giant Voice" base public address system booming out "ALARM RED MOPP 4", which meant that an attack was imminent. Sure enough there were missiles being fired into the Marine Corps border camps in Kuwait. It was scary as hell, especially since I was in a deep sleep. According to Fox News, there had been two missiles shot simultaneously, then another just minutes later. We were done wearing our gear, ready to go back to bed, and we had to jump up and put it on again.'

Attacks continued throughout the afternoon of 20 March, and Piggott recalled 'we were pounded every hour and a half or so with Scuds, getting up and putting on our stuff'. At times the alarms caught the 'Hounds' in embarrassingly inopportune situations. 'I was just in the shower, getting ready to go to work in the MPC, and the alarm went off again. I didn't get to shave or finish washing myself good enough – I only had my gas mask on and nothing else for a while', Piggott recounted. The following day, 'we were pounded eight times by Scud attacks, although I think two were false alarms. When I got back to the MPC, I found out that the last Scud impacted in the gulf due east of Jaber. It could have easily hit us.'

'PSYOPS' IS COMBAT TOO

While the Iraqis were striking back with potentially lethal Al Samouds, the 'Hounds' was dropping leaflets, as well as precision guided munitions, in return. Psychological warfare operations ('psyops') were a vital component of the Coalition's overall campaign plan, and the 524th FS was the only F-16 unit to participate.

Lt Col Pete Schaub (a very experienced fighter pilot with 2800 hours of fighter time, including 800 in the Viper, who had also flown F-111s, as well as RAF Harriers on exchange) was initially kept back at Cannon as the 'acting squadron commander', but once the die were cast he was brought forward, initially to head the unit's liaison team in the CAOC in Saudi Arabia. There, his desk was situated next to the USAF Public Affairs (PA) office, which assisted with the 'psyops' campaign, as well as reporting to the media. As Schaub said;

'They (PA) were planning the "Psyops" campaign and we were dropping their leaflet bombs, so it made sense to be next door to them. While initially not well received by the squadron as a "combat mission", it was one of those necessary evils in that the "psyops" part of OIF was as important as the actual kinetic destruction or kinetic effects of the war. But you don't get any feedback when you drop your weapons – nobody tells you if you got a hit or not, but I think everybody in the squadron accepted the fact that it was something that needed to be done.'

One of the young wingmen in the unit agreed, stating 'We all knew that it had to be done – it was the way we were trying to handle this whole war from the beginning. What was interesting with "psyops" was the fact that we were using old bombs to deliver the leaflets. The "weapons" had an old initiator and timer, which were very different to what we had been trained to drop. We therefore had to learn about how to drop this store "in the field", as we had never practised with manually steered and manually dropped bombs prior to deploying'.

Another pilot stated at the time, 'We have been dropping leaflets all over the place. Unfortunately, the "Hounds" have been carrying them all the way up to Baghdad, and been getting shot at in the process, all to carry paper. It seems a little unsafe to me, but that is what is helping make all the bad guys surrender'.

The 'Hounds'' maintenance troops tracked the number of bombs dropped by each of jet with yellow tally marks along the canopy sill. Here, Capt Chris Kurek shows off aircraft 88-0486's 27 bomb tally silhouettes. Never without his Chicago Cubs sun visor, Kurek was also one of the two 'Hounds' that made up the fighter pilot-troubadour duo called *'Dos Gringos'* (*USAF*)

These 'psyops' stores that they were expending were Mk 129 canisters (formerly used to deliver CBU bomblets) fitted with air-burst FMU-14 fuses to spread the PA papers across a large area.

Upon his return from the CAOC, Schaub led three leaflet-drop missions, putting into action the campaign he had watched – and assisted – PA develop. He went on to fly seven additional combat missions, dropping JDAM on airfields and against helicopters that had apparently been husbanded for Saddam Hussein's possible escape from Baghdad, as well as hitting Iraqi artillery with GBU-12s while dodging AAA. For this last mission – in extremely trying and adverse conditions – Schaub was awarded a DFC.

In addition to leading three 'leaflet bombing' missions, Lt Col Pete Schaub flew seven sorties that saw him drop more lethal ordnance. On one of the latter missions he dropped four GBU-12s on artillery that was disputing the Coalition's advance to Baghdad, earning a DFC in the process for pressing home his attacks in the face of heavy AAA (*Unofficial Squadron Yearbook*)

Maj Roberson helped orchestrate the USAF role in the 'psyops' mission from the CAOC, and he recalled one example where it was particularly effective. The ground campaigners wanted to neutralise the Iraqi 34th Armour Brigade on the flank of the advance without diverting Coalition forces from the drive to Baghdad. That unit was duly targeted for leaflet deliveries, as Roberson related. 'Two consecutive days of leaflets told them, "Hey! Your time's coming. Capitulate and lay down your arms, because if you don't then we're going to attack you". Since we had that capability and air superiority, that's what happened. After the bombing attack, we came back and dropped more leaflets that said, "We told you we'd do it. So, any of you guys that are left, go home!"'

The 34th Armour Brigade never showed up on the battlefield.

REAL BOMBS WORK EVEN BETTER

Despite understanding the necessity, and effectiveness, of showering leaflets upon the enemy, and having them go home instead of to the front, fighter pilots never liked these 'psyops' sorties, especially when compared with employing more destructive – and immediately persuasive – ordnance. A good example of the latter was a night time mission flown by Lt Col Kossler and his wingman, Capt Steve Strandburg.

'It was about a week into the war', Kossler explained, 'and the Army advance on Baghdad was bogged down in a brutal sandstorm. We were fragged for SCAR (strike coordination and reconnaissance) with JDAM aboard, and we took off out of Al Jaber. Often, we didn't tank, but we did on this particular mission. The weather was so bad up

Lt Col David Kossler (left) and Capt Steve Strandburg (right) were flying two of only six Coalition fighters airborne one night early on in the war when the rest of the Coalition's air operations – and its ground advance – had been halted by a lengthy and vicious sandstorm. Using GPS-guided GBU-31s, they hit Iraqi positions pinning down US troops. Kossler stated 'We made a lot of army guys happy that night' (*Unofficial Squadron Yearbook*)

north that the tankers were actually down south in Saudi Arabia. It was a dusk/night sortie in absolutely the worse weather I'd ever seen in my life. The tanker was up at 28,000 ft, dodging cumulus and thunderstorms. Armed with GBU-31 2000-lb JDAM, we were flying pretty heavy jets in afterburner in the thunderstorms, bouncing around'.

To get the wingman's perspective, Strandburg recalled, 'After a few sorties of either dropping my four leaflet bombs or nothing at all, I was beginning to get quite frus-

While the 'Hounds' were raining leaflets on Iraqi troops and civilians, the former often responded violently with AAA weapons such as this mobile ZPU-4. Discovered at Talil AB in southern Iraq, it is being examined here by the 524th's Intel Officer, Capt Jared Patrick. One of its four barrels now resides in the 524th FS's pilots' lounge at Cannon AFB (*Unofficial Squadron Yearbook*)

trated. However, one day we stepped to the jets and found two mighty JDAM hanging on the wings. Kossler and I briefed a Kill box Interdiction/Close Air Support mission due to the fact that we did not have specific targets to drop on. We expected to launch to the tanker track, refuel, and proceed to our assigned area and talk with the Army about what they needed us to eliminate.

'What happened was just that, except for extremely bad weather getting to and from the tanker track, coupled with the fact that this was our first night mission of the war. I was almost mentally drained just flying off of Kossler with NVGs to the tanker track. Once we joined up on the tanker, I fought spatial disorientation a few times.'

Kossler picks up the story. 'To get out of the bad weather area we had to fly in full afterburner just to climb above it. We ended up flying north to the target area from the tanker at above 45,000 ft in full afterburner. Fortunately, the fuel flow in 'burner at that altitude is not as high as it is when down low, so we were able to do it. We had enough fuel for one pass. Basically, the JTAC told us they were taking sporadic ground fire at their location, and they were requesting drops on these coordinates. So it was a JDAM delivery through the weather from 45,000 ft'.

Strandburg elaborated, 'After checking in with our GPS-guided munitions, the JTAC quickly informed us that his unit was taking fire from a nearby road intersection. Kossler asked if he could provide us with the exact location of the intersection, and the JTAC started reading us coordinates. We quickly inputted the location of the intersection into our mission computers and set up to drop 8000 lbs of "love" on the enemy, through the weather, at night.

'Shortly after showing a time of impact in my jet, the JTAC excitedly informed us that he heard the explosions nearby, and they were not taking fire anymore. I guess the attack destroyed the adversaries, or just scared the crap out of them. Either way, it was a great feeling to have helped out our Army brethren on the ground'.

Kossler added, 'We were basically the only ones that got any targets that night. There was a flight of F/A-18s – don't know who they were, or where they were from – and another "Hound" flight that "Saw" Bowman was leading with "Thumper" Hopper on his wing. We made a lot of Army guys happy, including our FAC, because he saw the explosions! They

Capt Charles Davis and Lt Chad Martin made an awesome 'combat pair' in OIF, with both pilots winning DFCs for their efforts to help the Army capture Baghdad International Airport by destroying Iraqi tanks and ammunition bunkers on the airfield. Here, flying off Davis' left wing, Martin is seen in the aircraft he used on that very mission (90-0744), loaded with two 2000-lb GBU-10s (*Chad Martin via Author*)

Lt Martin (left) and Capts Anthony Mulhare and Davis (right) pose with a 'bunker-busting' GBU-24 LGB. In addition to leading numerous missions, Davis was one of the 524th's two Weapons Instructors, who were responsible for preparing the 'Hounds' for combat. He did a fine job, as the unit's unprecedented 97.5 per cent weapons effectiveness clearly demonstrated (*Chad Martin via Author*)

were just thankful that anybody else was awake that night'.

A TALE OF TWO LIEUTENANTS

On 2 April Lt Chad Martin flew two memorable CAS missions, destroying Iraqi armour and other equipment as the Army's V Corps rapidly approached Baghdad from the southeast. 'On the first sortie of the day', he related, 'we were working near Baghdad with a FAC. Capt Davis talked me onto a tank, and then with the multiple number of missile launches in our general direction – one split our formation off my right wingtip by less than 500 ft – we decided to leave the area.

'We then started working with a FAC on the outskirts of Baghdad. He talked us onto some vehicles covered with camouflaged netting. Davis took out several of them, and then passed me the lead to take out a couple more. The heaviest missile activity was mainly over the heart of the city, and most of them were SA-2/3s that were launched ballistically, trying to be the "golden BB". If we stayed on the outskirts, it wasn't so bad, but the haze of the burning tyres – a primitive concealment tactic by the defending Iraqis – made it harder to locate the vehicles.'

After returning to Al Jaber for more bombs, Martin and Davis immediately received tasking for their second sortie. The Army was getting close to Baghdad now, and combat raged intensely as the troops approached the enemy capital. Lt Martin continued;

'For our second mission we were fragged to go up and work a kill box south of Baghdad. Having seen a lot of missile activity on the first mission, we were a little concerned when they told us to "push secure" on the encrypted KY-58 VHF radios. We were quickly informed that we had been re-fragged to work Baghdad International Airport, killing anything that could possibly be military on or near the airport.

'We were armed with four slant-mounted GBU-12s apiece – slant-mounted meant that we were carrying two GBU-12s on each side of the jet on a triple ejector rack (TER). Because of the constraints of the fuel tanks and the expanding fins on the GBU-12, we couldn't carry one on the inboard station of the TER. Hence two bombs on the TER instead of three. The configuration we carried them in saw an LGB on the bottom and one on the outer rack, giving them a slanted look when hanging on the jet. That,

or two GBU-31 JDAM, was our normal load-out for the first couple of weeks of OIF.

'We hit a tanker before going into Baghdad. As we took up position over the airport, the smoke haze from the tyre burning was extremely thick. There were also missile launches in our immediate vicinity. Davis found some munitions storage bunkers when he spied a series of suspicious looking "spots" along both sides of the runway. They were definitely military targets, based on their shape and set up, but we didn't know exactly what they were until he hit one of them. The site of "cooking off" ammo soon confirmed the bunkers' contents.

'While Davis was finding targets and rolling in, I flew cover, which is basically an extension of the "fighting wing" – the "wedge position" to be exact. You're in a cone at his "six o'clock" for one to three miles. Your main job is to look out in the target area for any kind of threats, do belly checks, because we are almost constantly in a turn, and check the radar for contacts off the nose.

'As he rolled in on one pass, there was a SAM launch across his nose. After directing him to break, I prepared to take a mark and roll in on the site that had shot at Davis. He instructed me not to roll in and drop on them because he thought it might be a SAM trap, so I took a mark and immediately passed up the coordinates to AWACS. We then left the area to let it cool off.

'The ammo bunkers Davis had hit near the runway were still exploding when we came back 15 minutes later! Thankfully, the Iraqis almost always placed anything of military value in a revetment, making it fairly easy to identify potential targets. We flew over the area and started searching through the "revets" for hot spots, or unusual shapes that looked like something other than dirt. We then proceeded to strike the tanks we found in the "revets". I killed three tanks before hitting Bingo with one bomb left. Davis took out the ammo storage areas and a tank.

'That evening, and into the next morning, V Corps moved in and took the airport. I remember that mission the most, not because I got the DFC for it, but because it put all of the things I had achieved in OSW/OIF together for me. I was responsible for my Flight lead's safety, and actually had to be directive. There was a lot of shooting going on that day, and a

A jubilant Lt Martin returns from a mission in aircraft 90-0744. This jet was actually assigned to Capt Davis – during OIF all crew names were removed from the canopy rails as an operations security measure – but was flown mostly by Martin. Fittingly, following Davis' departure from the unit, 90-0744 was assigned to Martin for the duration of his assignment with the 524th FS (*USAF*)

lot of it seemed aimed at us. I actually used my training and tools successfully, took out some tanks and saw the fruits of our labour by watching V Corps roll into the airport on Fox News before I went to bed that night. It was gratifying knowing that I had played a small part in helping them to do that.'

Martin eventually flew 29 OIF missions – a high mark for a short war – logged almost 100 hours of combat time and dropped nearly 40,000 lbs of munitions – two GBU-10s, 11 GBU-12s, 14 JDAM and four Mk 129 leaflet bombs.

THE SECOND LIEUTENANT

Lt Mark Johnson still wore his MQT moniker of 'Pup-J'. Like all USAF fighter units, the 'Hounds' do not name a new squadron member until he/she passes his/her Mission Ready (MR) checkride. Until then, the new 524th pilot is not a 'Hound', but a mere 'Pup', and is so designated by the suffix of their surname initial. Thus Johnson was 'Pup-J' until his naming, which followed the conflict. Now-Capt Mark Johnson is known as 'Magic' in reference to some of his amazing feats at the controls of the Viper in OIF.

Johnson was the newest of the new 'Hounds', having arrived at the 524th FS on 24 August 2002 and passed his MR check on 17 December. From the outset, he knew this squadron meant business;

'My first experience here was when I came in and met the DO, Lt Col Givens, who is a gung ho, going-to-war kinda guy. And so we're having our brief, and told me 'I want you to be ready. As soon as MQT is over you need to be ready to go to war immediately'. And just to show me how serious he was, he pulled his "hit-and-run" bag out from under his desk. He could have left the minute we were talking if they said, "Get on an airplane and go".

'So from that point on I knew that all these years of OSW were coming to an end. These smart lieutenant colonels had a good handle on this, and the squadron was probably going to be deployed to the Middle East before we knew it.'

Joining the squadron in-theatre in mid-March 2003, Johnson was initially sent to the CAOC to assist Lt Col Pete Schaub, and they returned on the 30th, ready to do their part. He was immediately reminded of the deadly seriousness of being ready for combat. As Johnson described it;

'I showed up there, and I'm eating dinner – everybody was on their own schedule – by myself. All of a sudden Lt Col Givens sat down right in front of me and said, "You ready to fly tomorrow morning?" "Yes, sir." "You think you're studied up on everything?" "Yes, sir." "Well, you're gonna be flying with the boss, TST – they are the guys who have been getting the most action, so be ready." It was interesting to walk into that the very next morning. We sat TST and I flew twice that morning!'

Lt Col Berghoff (left), who was the 524th FS CO in OIF, continued the age old tradition of USAF fighter squadron commanders by flying with the youngest wingman in the unit in combat. Here, he poses with wingman Lt Mark Johnson, who was so new that he had not even been given his 'tactical call-sign' by the time OIF came around (*Unofficial Squadron Yearbook*)

So, on the morning of 31 March, sitting TST Alert with a pair of 2000-lb JDAM-guided BLU-109s beneath his wings, Johnson would get a chance to do what he had been trained to do. The two-ship was soon scrambled to attack Iraqi leadership targets in Karbala as 'Kismet 21/22'. Johnson explained what happened next;

'My first mission in OIF was right after I came back from the CAOC, when I sat alert on Lt Col Berghoff's wing. I dropped two JDAM penetrators into Baath Party bunkers – that was the first time I had ever expended live weapons, and I was in combat! It felt like I was dropping a Volkswagen off of each wing! There was no doubt that the bomb had left!

'There wasn't any direct threat to us at that time. We were flying high, of course, for the JDAM. We dropped them and turned and started running back towards Kuwait. As the wingman, I remember wanting to see where those bombs "splashed", so I was banking the jet up left and right, trying – in vain – to see down behind me where they were hitting. Even with the targeting pod I couldn't see anything because they exploded beneath the earth. When we came back and watched the video on a bigger TV, we could see where they had gone into two different holes. I remember thinking to myself, "Wow, they're in there!"'

Johnson had little time to reflect on his success, however. Before the debriefing was complete, the TST alert jets had been re-armed with GBU-31 JDAM and scrambled (again as 'Kismet 21/22') to hit targets in the centre of Baghdad. The pilots received the target coordinates en route to the Iraqi capital and, disbelieving them, checked and rechecked them several times;

'I started plotting it on the map, and this TST was taking us right into the middle of Baghdad! We found out that we were after an SA-2 site. We dropped our bombs on it, turned, and as we headed home we saw the bombs hit. That was when the SA-2 cooked off. Through the targeting

F-16CG 88-0528 dropped more ordnance than any other 524th EFS Viper in OIF, some 44 yellow bomb symbols eventually being marked along its canopy sill. These included four for the quartet of 2000-lb GBU-31s dropped by Lt Mark Johnson on the Baath Party headquarters in Karbala and an SA-2 site in Baghdad (*Unofficial Squadron Yearbook*)

pod that is looking back behind us, the SAM appeared to be coming right up after us. It had a spiral effect. In the video you saw this big spiralling smoke trail coming up towards us. We were both rather alarmed by it, although at least it wasn't guided. The missile was just "cooking off".'

Although he had arrived late to the shooting war, Lt Johnson racked up an impressive tally in the few remaining days of the conflict – 14 sorties flown and almost 10,000 lbs of ordnance dropped. Two days after his initial experience, he got to use his very first LGB, destroying a tank in a revetment. The following day he used another GBU-12 to target a large fuel truck that was also parked in a revetment, Johnson reporting;

'It blew up, and then just down the road something else exploded. We think it must have been the fuel pump – an underground fuel line that was used to refuel all their vehicles in that particular area.'

HUNTING FOR 'CHEMICAL ALI'

'Today I targeted the Iraqi regime – the very reason we started this war.' So reads Lt Piggott's journal entry for 5 April. 'It was pretty awesome, just like out of a movie. Maj Dewey and I were sitting alert, and we were told that in several hours we would have a very juicy target. It turns out we were going to hunt for "Chemical Ali" (Gen Ali Hassan al-Majeed), Saddam's cousin in charge of the chemical weapons programme in Iraq for many years. He had tortured thousands of people and killed even more with chemical weapons in the Iran/Iraq War and against the Kurds. He is one of the most feared people in that country. We were told that guys on the ground had watched him all day and found where he was going to be, and they were waiting for us to go and get him'.

Lt Col Berghoff confirmed that in addition to directly supporting the advance to Baghdad, his 'Hounds' were also occasionally tasked with helping to fulfil the principle objective of the campaign – the forcible, and if necessary, lethal removal of Iraq's leadership. As he said, 'through the CAOC and Intelligence, we were tasked against high-value targets. These were high-value leadership targets, both fleeting and mobile, that had to be struck immediately or we may have lost the opportunity'.

Lt Piggott continued;

'It was 0400 hrs before we were allowed to go out there and crank our jets. The word from the mission director was to scramble, call the guys on the ground as soon as we got airborne and get cleared to drop. That is what we did, and it was going to be exciting. We took off just before dawn, with the sun creating an orange halo on the horizon. We cruised to Basra, only about 90 miles north of our base, to check it out and get a "hack" (information) on where the target was going to be in our pods. The coordinates we were given were spot on, and my pod was looking right at where it was supposed to.

One of the primary tasks of the 'Hounds' was the forcible removal of the Iraqi leadership regime. Thus, Lt Russ Piggott personally addressed this LGB directly to its target audience, but the bomb was actually used against a radar site during an eight-ship 'Hound' attack on Al Asad airfield. The latter was a huge base northwest of Baghdad that was home to the IrAF's MiG-25 'Foxbat' force. It is now the primary Marine Corps air base in Iraq (*Unofficial Squadron Yearbook*)

The 'Hounds'' weapon of choice was the laser-guided 500-lb GBU-12. Having precision targeting and surgical destructive power, it was favoured for its ability to take out small targets without damaging surrounding civilian structures. Having dropped a total of 377 GBU-12s, the 524th EFS ran its stocks of 500-lb LGBs so low that it was eventually forced to ration itself to just two bombs (instead of four) per jet (*Unofficial Squadron Yearbook*)

'Upon checking in with the 'snake eaters' (British SAS) on the ground, they told us we were cleared to drop. There were multiple threats in the area – SA-9, SA-13, ZSU-23-4, S-60 and other anti-aircraft weapons. There was a cloud deck at about 15,000 ft north of the target, but to the south it was clear.

'It was good to get a look at the target when we first got up there because this would help us when it came to dropping these buildings. We were targeting his house right in downtown Basra, along one of the canals. I had studied the picture of what we were going to hit so well it was imprinted on my brain. We were to drop the second and third buildings, leaving the others untouched. My DMPI (desired mean point of impact) was the distinct square top on the third building. Our GBU-12, fitted with 0.25-millisecond delay fusing, would let the bomb go in the house about 20 ft then explode inside, crushing it from within, but sparing the stuff to the sides.

'We captured the target area on-screen and pressed in for our first attack run – it was easy to see the target, and I was pretty excited. I was on the left and Dewey on the right. We were to drop simultaneously so that our lasers were not obscured by any of the dust from the explosion caused by the other guy's bomb. If they were released and impacted within one second of each other it would not be a problem. Anything other than that would cause guidance difficulties.

'Our timing was perfect. I let my bomb go and looked over to Dewey – his was on its way too. We cranked right and finessed our targeting pods on the aim points. Mine was surprisingly easy to keep on target, and I knew for sure it was going to be a success. The bomb entered the building on the second floor street side and exited through the back porch, leaving a gaping hole in the front and a huge plume of dust in the back yard – it was a dud! I was so pissed, but Dewey's bomb didn't even show up. It had not guided, fell well short of the target and blew up in the street two blocks away.

'We had to come around for a re-attack, and quickly, as we didn't want the people inside to get away. As I looked down at the target area, there were many flashes coming from below, right in the centre of the city. It was high-speed flashing and not coming up that far at us so I wasn't too worried. On the second attack, I told Dewey that I was five seconds from release, and just as the bomb thunked away he said "don't drop". It was too late. The bomb guided perfectly, impacting just where the cursors were, on the hole from the first one, and dropping the whole building. It was flattened, but the house to the side of it still remained.

'Dewey re-attacked again, but this time his bomb went about 300 metres too long, right into the middle of a neighbourhood on the other side of the canal – oops. This left his whole building still standing. We made two more passes for him and they both hit the mark, crushing that place and everything inside of it. They were flat, but the "snake eaters" wanted another one, so I would have to drop again. I hit the back half of Dewey's building, exploding a cloud of dust and debris all over the place. It was beautiful to watch from the targeting pod.

'When we made our pass over it for battle damage assessment (BDA), it was clear it was success. What was not a success was the fact that three of the seven bombs didn't hit the target, and it took us 20 minutes to do what should have taken us two passes and five minutes.

'When we got back and looked at the tapes, it was great footage. On my second bomb – the one that actually exploded – there was a walker in the street that had been strolling all the way up the block, and someone runs out of Dewey's target house just about a second before the bomb explodes. The walker was definitely killed, but the other individual I am not sure about, and I really hope that it was not "Chemical Ali", because if he got away I will definitely be pissed off.'

Two days later, Capt Al Lockwood, a spokesman for the British military at US CENTCOM HQ, reported 'the body of Gen Ali Hassan al-Majeed has been found'. At the Pentagon, Gen Richard Myers, Chairman of the Joint Chiefs of Staff, was using Lt Piggott's targeting pod video to illustrate SecDef Rumsfeld's comment 'We believe that the reign of terror of "Chemical Ali" has come to an end'.

In the event, however, this proved not to be the case. While one of Ali's bodyguards was killed – and the planning meeting of 78 Iraqi officers was definitely broken up – the malfunctioning bombs of the first pass signalled imminent danger, and "Chemical Ali" had just enough time to get away before the second pass. He was eventually captured by Coalition forces on 17 August 2003 – well after the completion of OIF I. But in the meantime, Piggott was definitely 'pissed off'!

By early-April the 524th EFS was running out of 500-lb GBU-12s, so it had to start carrying the much heavier 2000-lb GBU-10, with a commensurately larger blast damage area. By that time, however, the Army was engaged in urban combat, and it did not want the larger bombs used, since the troops were in close combat in the very tight confines of Baghdad and other major cities. Nevertheless, the 524th FS, operating at the leading edge of the battle front, had truly done a magnificent job. As squadron commander Lt Col Tom Berghoff summed up;

'I am extremely proud of the squadron's accomplishments. We had a lot of guys that were young – without much experience out on the wing – that did just great. They did really well because my flight leads did what they were supposed to. They led the flights, made the right decisions and took their wingmen and got them in and out of Iraq, and the end result was a 100 per cent mission success rate. All the targets were positively ID'd as military, and there were no collateral damage issues – there was no fratricide by

'Hounds" jets were also armed with the deep-penetrating 2000-lb GBU-24 LGB. However, the squadron used only two of these in combat, and both were expended during a four-ship mission led by Lt Col Berghoff. He and Capt Jeremy Quataker dropped them on MiG fighters that the Iraqis had buried near a town. A third MiG spotted uncovered in a ditch was destroyed when Quataker strafed it. By early April stocks of GBU-12s were running low at Al Jaber, and the jets were armed with the 2000-lb GBU-10s and GBU-24s instead. The much larger blast damage area of these weapons limited their employment opportunities, leaving the more heavily armed jets to sit out the final stages of OIF when urban CAS was very much the order of the day (*USAF*)

All boasting lengthy yellow bomb tallies beneath their cockpits, four 524th EFS F-16CGs perform a formation flyby over Al Jaber AB on 30 April 2003. A few days later the unit ended its marathon OSW/OIF tour and returned home to Cannon AFB (*Capt Ed Bahret*)

Few of the distinctive bomb tally markings survive today. Aircraft 88-0510 still proudly bears mission markings in an acceptably subdued Air Combat Command way, its 41 bomb silhouettes visual evidence of the outstanding job done by all the 'Hounds' – pilots, maintainers, weapons troops, support personnel and the F-16CGs themselves – in OIF (*Author's Collection*)

the squadron. Pilots made the right decisions, threat-reacted to survive and had no battle damage.

'We flew a lot of sorties and worked hard. We didn't miss one of our TST taskings, and a lot of that was quick reaction, quick thinking. When things happen fast, there is a tendency to make mistakes, but they didn't. We blew up a lot of high value targets and supported the Army's push to Baghdad. And we brought everybody home.'

Berghoff has every reason to be proud of his 'Hounds'. Collectively they dropped 372 500-lb GBU-12s, 23 2000-lb GBU-10s, two deep penetrating GBU-24s, 244 GBU-31 JDAM, 108 Mk 129 leaflet bombs and fired 568 rounds 20 mm PGU-28 ammunition – some 724,000 lbs of ordnance – and they did so with an outstanding 97.5 per cent weapons effectiveness. This ordnance was used to destroy 69 tanks and armoured vehicles, 44 artillery pieces, 82 trucks and assorted soft-skin vehicles, 47 command, control and communications targets, 35 Iraqi Army barracks and weapons storage sites, 14 SAMs, radars and AAA pieces and 14 aircraft. The unit's maintainers and weapons troops generated 597 sorties, flying a total of 1438 combat hours during OIF.

At the time of this writing it was announced that Cannon AFB was on the SecDef's list for base closures in the 2006-2010 time frame. What will become of the 27th FW and 524th FS 'Hounds of Heaven' is currently known only in the halls of the Pentagon. They could be reassigned to some other base, or be closed completely and the flags furled, awaiting a time when national need requires another expansion of the USAF. If so, the outstandingly effective combat record of the 524th FS in OIF will pass into the history books, creating a great legacy for any future 'Hounds of Heaven' to draw upon when they activate and live up to should they go to war.

410TH AEW

'I was flying wing for Maj Ned Linch. We were on a night mission as "Honcho 23/24", flying reconnaissance over possible Scud hiding sites. It was Day 10 of the war (30 March), and the weather was awful', recalled Capt Brian Wolf. His section mate, Maj Linch, elaborated, 'The weather was thick clouds from 25,000 ft down to around 10,000 ft, with ragged bottoms, and visibility below the weather was a real problem. The haze and sand in the air made for a no-horizon, milk bowl, effect. It was also difficult to see the ground with NVGs since there was zero illumination – no moon, stars or cultural lighting'.

'You just couldn't see a thing. It was the most uncomfortable time that I've ever spent in the jet', Wolf stated without a hint of a smile. Linch and Wolf were flying ATO mission number 4523.

Linch, a Delta Airlines pilot and activated Guardsman, and Wolf, a former enlisted trooper, are 'F-16C+' pilots with the Alabama ANG. In the final hour of 'Honcho' flight's assigned vulnerability period, they were proceeding north from the tanker looking for likely hiding places for TBMs. As the two continued north, Linch recalled that they received a radio call from 'Bondo' (the RAF AWACS controller) to contact 'Vader', which it later became clear was a squad of British SOF troops in jeopardy;

'"Bondo" vectored us north and gave us coordinates and a couple of TAD frequencies, but no one replied. Then "Velcro" – a two-ship of F-16s from the 160th FS with no tasking for tanker support – came up on our Victor (VHF) frequency, in the clear (unsecured), and told us that "Vader" was on UHF Guard. We pushed to that frequency and talked to "Vader".'

What they heard from 'Vader' would stay with them both forever;

'We heard a guy yelling for help, and there's no doubt from the tone of his voice that he needed it right now. I get the shivers every time I think about that call, and the sound of his voice', Wolf recalled.

And with the benefit of the actual voice tape from that night, Linch relived the experience;

'There was a calm voice and there was an hysterical voice. They were calling, "Fast Air, Fast Air! We are completely surrounded! The enemy around our position (heavy breath-

ing) have turned out all lights", then, "Fast Air, Fast Air! We need your help!" "Okay, what do you need from us? Do you want us to do strobe on?" (heavy breathing with a frantic voice). And then they said, "Everything around us within 300 metres, totally destroy. We are completely surrounded and they have all lights out!".'

Despite the gravity of the situation, and the frantic calls from the SOF guys on the ground, Linch and Wolf's replies to 'Vader' were calm and measured, and they gave a sense of hope. 'There has not been a day go by since', Linch added, 'that I do not think about this mission, and the voices of that one SOF guy calling for help. It was that frantic, hysterical, voice that drew us into the fight. It was our "calling" to press the limits – we disregarded concern for ourselves and pushed beyond the boundaries of our jets and our personal limitations'.

The SOF squad was under fire somewhere in the Al Jezera desert of western Iraq. 'This was considered a high-threat mission for them, but high gain', Linch remarked, 'and their non-covert route between Al Qaim and Mosul took them near Subaikha airfield'. The men, of whom there were 52 in total, had been inserted two nights before and were split into two groups separated by a few kilometres. Having made initial contact with tribal leaders and handed out cigarettes and tea to the region's Bedouin, they had moved to a secure harbour area in the desert. Unbeknownst to them, the Bedouin had swapped sides, and as the SOF squads progressed across the desert in their vehicles, the Iraqi Army was planning to ambush them. Wolf continued;

'They were being chased, fleeing in their Range Rovers and other vehicles into nearby foothills. Over the radio you could hear fire being exchanged every time the FAC keyed his mic, and to make matters worse, the SOF were spread out, some to the east and some to the west'. 'Vader' had been alone, fighting a well-armed, vehicle-borne, Iraqi force of some 500 men for two hours without support.

'We had a 9000-ft (mean sea level) overcast, and the elevation out to the west was about 2000-3000 ft, so we had no more than 7000 ft in which to work. We had to get in below the cloud to be effective, but Gen Moseley has been very specific about the 10,000-ft hard deck, and guys had been getting into trouble for going below it. We had no choice, however', Wolf explained. 'We broke through the weather at 7000 ft, knowing full well that we could be in trouble, but as long as there were guys on the ground who needed us, we didn't care'.

Linch's game plan was to make a series of bomb passes from a ten-mile pattern, where he could point at the target area, start a descent from below 10,000 ft using a bunt manoeuvre, fly at tactical airspeed and offset from their position for an unguided GBU-12 delivery into the dark in a bid to thwart the enemy. 'This was the best tactic for the situation', he concluded. 'The weather was too marginal to fly visual tactics, so offset bombing was the only solution based on the urgent situation. I also planned to use flares in case of an IR SAM attack'.

By now Wolf has assumed a two-mile trail formation on Linch, who 'had his anti-collision light on in the covert lighting NVG mode so the guys on the ground couldn't see it. We were trying to determine where these friendlies were, where the bad guys were and where we need to put our bombs. It was chaos, pure chaos. Guys were everywhere, we didn't

Maj Ned Linch carried these extra items as part of his survival kit on every combat mission. 'The family photo was recommended because they might have sympathy on you when it came to beatings, since families are seen as equally important to the Iraqis' (*Ned Linch*)

Looking over the right wing of this 160th EFS Viper over western Iraq, this aircraft is armed with two slant-configured GBU-12s and an AMRAAM, but no AIM-9M (*Ned Linch*)

know who was talking on the radio, or what his position was, and we were trying to find them with the pod and our NVGs. But there was zero light, so the NVGs were only good for picking up ground fire and the anti-collision light of Linch's jet. It was hard to pinpoint "Vader's" location because he wouldn't give us his coordinates over the radio.

'He told us he had a "firefly" that he was holding up above his head. A "firefly" was a nine-volt battery with a little inch-by-half-inch capped bulb that worked for covert NVGs, but couldn't be seen with the naked eye. So there we were well below the RoE floor, flying in this haze down low at 400-500 knots because we didn't want to get hit by a MANPAD or AAA, and we knew approximately where "Vader" was, and we were looking for this "firefly". It was becoming very frustrating because the SOF guys were on the run, being fired at, and weren't in a position to slow down and tell us where they were. You could see bursts of small arms fire being exchanged in the darkness, but we just couldn't do anything to help out.'

Linch picked up the story;

'The washing out of my goggles by the MFDs and the cockpit lighting made it almost impossible to pick out their strobe in the desert "dark hole". So, I turned all my lights in the cockpit down or off and dimmed my MFDs and HUD as low as possible. I stayed oriented by using the HUD and a very dimly lit attitude indicator (ADI), but was counting on Wolf to crosscheck my altitude!'

Despite repeated dry runs over the target coordinates in his blacked-out cockpit, Linch was unable to release a GBU-12 because he could only visually acquire the 'firefly' at the very last minute. Wolf, covering his lead for threats, and calling out altitudes lest Linch became fixated with finding the SOF soldiers and flew into the ground, had more luck;

'I suddenly saw a "firefly". It was just a faint little blink, and I split from my lead and anchored a turn around where this little blink was – it was just plain luck that I spotted it. In the meantime, there was an AC-130 inbound about 100 miles out, and it was going to take him a

Rob Ray heads east into Iraq in 88-0399, which was the wing commander's jet in OIF. The aircraft's well known viper tail flash was removed prior to the unit going into combat for the first time (*Ned Linch*)

while to arrive on-scene. I told him to anchor ten miles south of our coordinates, and then we'd hand-off the job to him so that he could come in and clean up – he was slower and more vulnerable than us, but he could do a better job, and had a lot more firepower at his disposal. But, for the moment, we were the only ones there that could help these guys out.'

Linch handed Wolf the 'tactical' lead because 'Honcho 24' was in a better position to make an effective attack. The latter recalled;

'I anchored over the "firefly", and all I was doing was flying visually over this little "straw of hope". By this point we had been here for 20 minutes, and had had to listen in frustration to guys calling for help over the radio. I confirmed "Vader's" location and asked him where the enemy was, but I couldn't understand what he was saying in reply. I tried to be proactive, and helped him by saying "are there any friendlies north of your position?" "Negative, no friendlies", he replied. "Where is the enemy in reference to you?" I asked. "They are north and northeast", he confirmed. Well, we were finally getting somewhere.

'This was all happening at a high-pitch, high-octane level, and I said to him, "I am visual with your position. If I drop a 500-lb bomb three-clicks (three kilometres north of your position), confirm that I am well clear of all friendlies". He replied that I will be, so I reconfirmed it, then I reconfirmed his position and reconfirmed the location of the other friendlies. I added a little bit to the "three clicks" to make it about "four-five clicks", then I rolled into a 30-degree dive and pickled a GBU-12 in a dumb bomb release – not guiding, just falling to the northeast to give the guys on the ground something to help me with target guidance. The bomb hit and I was off target with flares at about 5000 ft.

'As soon as I had pulled away "Vader" called, "Contact explosion and contact your flares". I replied "Copy. In relation to the last bomb, where does the next bomb need to go?" We had now established a point of reference, and the tone in his voice became calmer and things seemed to immediately turn around in his favour. At this point it sounded like the SOF troops had left their vehicles behind and were rapidly egressing to the south.'

'Frustrated with our inability to maintain contact with the troops, and the potential for fratricide, we utilised flares a few times to help disrupt the enemy troops. We received the call "Visual your chaff" in response. The only problem with this tactic was that the flares highlighted our position, and also blinded us, forcing us to recover the jet from unusual attitudes in a blacked-out cockpit with a dimly lit ADI', Linch continued.

'Shortly after "Honcho 24's" attack, I noticed more lights on the ground, indicating to me that we were making a difference. Our noise, flares and the single GBU-12 had given the friendlies the chance to escape and terminate the "Sprint" – the codename for guys on the ground whose lives were in danger.'

Before departing the target area, Linch confirmed with 'Vader' that the SOF 'Sprint' was indeed over, and then egressed the target area to proceed back to the tanker for more fuel. 'Honcho' flight then offered the British troops additional support, but it was not required. Linch recalled, 'They were still talking, but just not at the hysterical level they were when we arrived. I was concerned about their fate because I thought they had lost men in the "Sprint", and would almost certainly lose some more in the exfiltration'.

AC-130 'Slayer 55' arrived on-scene and Linch passed them control before declaring Bingo fuel and heading with Wolf back to Jordan. On the hour-long flight home, the two discussed their performance over their intra-flight frequency, and the burning question of 'who were those guys?' came back time and again. Linch admitted;

'I thought we had probably lost a lot of men in this battle. I was frustrated and down. I've never shed tears after an F-16 flight, but this night I did. I thought the SOF team had not made it, and that our actions had been ineffective.'

Wolf was also desperate for news;

'Every day thereafter I ask the British SOF liaison guy in the command post about the guys on the ground, and he said "no word yet". About a week later he told me that it turned out that there were 54 guys on the ground – all of them from the Royal Navy's Special Boat Service (SBS). The AC-130 had flown cover for some Chinooks that came and picked these guys up, but as they got some 20 miles west of the rendezvous point, they found out that they had left 12 guys behind. One of the Chinooks turned around to pick them up, but could only find ten of them. It turned out that the other two had jumped into a four-wheeler and headed west.'

Linch and Wolf would go on to jointly receive the Joe Bill Dryden Semper Viper Award for airmanship skills from Lockheed Martin in 2003, and Linch also received the DFC with the Valor device for his part in leading this mission. Finally, Linch was chosen by the Chief of Staff of the USAF, Gen Jumper, as the 2003 Aviation Valor Award Winner. He was presented with his award by the American Legion Aviators' Post 743 in New York City in May 2004.

But this sortie was atypical of those that were being flown by the 160th EFS at the time. As Wolf put it, 'Our mission was Scud busting for the western AO of Iraq – we were pretty much reconnaissance platforms, but we did fly CAS and the Offensive Counter-

This photograph of a physically drained Maj Ned Linch was taken immediately after he had landed back at Azraq following his frantic 30 March 2003 flight as 'Honcho 23' (*Ned Linch*)

Now-Lt Col Linch (right) and his wingman, now-Maj Brian 'Wolfman' Wolf (left), jointly received the coveted Joe Bill Dryden Semper Viper Award for 2003 following their exploits in OIF. Linch has over 3000 hours in the F-16 and the F-111 (*Ned Linch*)

Air role too'. Anti-Scud sorties were officially known as Counter-Theatre Ballistic Missile (C-TBM) missions .

To understand the 410th AEW's mission fully, one needs to go back to January 2003. Situated in modest facilities at Montgomery Regional Airport, Alabama, the 160th FS/187th FW is an inconspicuous ANG unit without airs or graces. But closer inspection reveals that this is little more than a façade, for the 160th operates perhaps the most advanced and capable F-16s in US service.

'We have, in the past five years, tended to get all the new toys that have come out', added Wolf. 'We were one of the first units to get NVGs, GBU-31s and SADL (situational awareness data link) too. The ANG bureau has directed them to us because we are a good wing with a good track record. We were lucky that we had been given the bombs and assets to be a leading ANG unit, and that culminated in us all of a sudden being the most capable MDS platform available. This was an unusual situation for us, as the ANG is usually behind the active duty (AD) Air Force. One of the primary reasons as to why this was the case was the fact that the ANG bureau could cut through red tape and get its acquisitions a lot easier than the AD'.

This fact was not lost on the planners responsible for engineering OIF, and it came as no surprise, therefore, when in January 2003 this tight-knit unit was notified that it was to be ready for deployment to fight the war in Iraq. The Alabama ANG would be tasked with two of the most important missions of the war – Scud hunting and SOF support. Perhaps more than any other Viper unit to deploy to OIF, the 187th FW's experiences and achievements would prove nothing short of exceptional.

Under the command of Col Stanley Clarke, the Alabama ANG swung into action. It would be deployed to Azraq AB, Jordan, and would be augmented *in situ* by men and women from the Colorado and Washington DC ANGs. The Colorado ANG would deploy 12 aircraft, but the Washington DC ANG would leave its 'small mouth' F-16s behind so that maintenance could be simplified by limiting ramp space to only those Vipers with 'big mouths' (GE F110 engines). Combined, they would form the 410th AEW.

Clarke, following a personal telephone request from Gen Moseley in October 2002, would be the overall wing commander, and he would run an operation comprised not only of F-16s, but also of Predator UAV drones, A-10s and a total of 3300 people. Air Force Reserve F-16C Block 30s from the 466th FS at Hill AFB, Utah, would also join the wing, its six jets arriving at Azraq following the completion of the unit's AEF VII deployment to PSAB.

Clarke's maintenance troops performed flawlessly in preparing the 160th FS jets for war, bringing forward planned PHASE inspections to ensure that each aircraft would be ready to fly uninterrupted combat missions once in-theatre. Every weapons armourer was also qualified pre-war to load the full array of munitions at the wing's disposal.

The pilots set to work preparing for the mission. Four visited Nellis AFB – home to an extensive collection of foreign weapons systems – and studied the Scud extensively. Others spent hours pre-visualising what the Scud would look like in the targeting pod from different ranges, altitudes and angles.

Arriving at Azraq on 13 February provided the Alabama residents with a host of culture shocks and challenges to overcome. There were no facilities on base for them to use – no water, no food hall, no sanitation – nothing. The wing quickly set about building its own facilities, erecting tents, a command centre, an MPC building, billeting and latrines. Looking through a photo album from one of the pilots that was there at the time, the scope of their task becomes immediately obvious. To top it all off, these facilities were built under a 24-hour threat of sniper fire from the base perimeter!

Left, below and bottom
Building the operations and living quarters from the ground up required a 100 per cent effort from each and every person deployed. Pictured here in sequence is the construction process for a relaxation room: 1) build the framework; 2) nail together; and 3) furnish with recliners! (*160th FS via Scott Patten*)

Clarke characterised the 410th AEW as 'almost a separate task force in some respects. In fact, there was some talk about that being exactly what we would officially become'. This mentality makes sense, particularly when one compares this wing with many of the other Viper units in-theatre. Other OIF F-16 pilots make mention of a lack of ground liaison support or coordination for much of the war, but the 410th AEW had SOF ground liaison officers in place for the entire conflict, and its pilots were destined from the start to work in very close proximity with the enigmatically-named Task Force 20 (TF-20).

Indeed, it was for this very reason that Clarke had despatched a small cadre of pilots to Nellis prior to deployment to practice C-TBM tactics with SOF observers on the ground, and his newly-equipped SADL 'F-16C+s' relied on a limited-range ground transmitter carried in the back of an SOF HMMWV all-terrain vehicle. The latter would be embedded with TF-20 patrols as they roamed western Iraq searching for leadership targets, communication nodes and TBMs.

This system, know as BUG-E (Battlefield Universal Gateway Equipment), allowed the TF-20 commander to transmit a host of data to nearby SADL-equipped F-16s so that they could attack enemy targets – or defend friendlies – based on the accurate GPS-derived data it supplied. Critically, this same information was broadcast to the CAOC, where the planners could watch events unfold in real time. The SADL/BUG-E combination would ultimately prove invaluable in the 160th EFS's NTISR mission.

Settled in as best they could, the three ANG units and single Reserve squadron now had a total of 40 F-16s in-theatre. Lt Col William Sparrow, who was the 410th AEW's scheduler, explained how the flying operations were divided up;

The Colorado ANG's 120th FS deployed with 12 of its F-16Cs to Azraq (*S Brown*)

This Alabama ANG jet features the unit's initial OIF mission load-out of four GBU-12s in slant configuration. Note that the pairs of bombs are actually carried on TERs, and that these GBU-12s feature the revised seeker head used until stocks in-theatre ran out. The seeker heads seen here are supposed to offer slightly superior performance (*160th FS via Scott Patten*)

'The Hill guys ran their own show, and so did the aircrew from Colorado. The reservists arrived about a week after we did. There were fewer DC guys, and they were split in half and divided up amongst the other squadrons. We shared the jets, though – I would go out to fly, and it could be a Colorado or Hill jet, or one of ours. What's more interesting is that the Hill guys, who had been in-theatre for over a month, had also been sharing jets with the Texas ANG and a second unit. So, when they showed up they brought other fin flashes with them. We ended up with a real a mixture of tails on the ramp. The DC squadron commander became the Operational Support Squadron boss, and the Colorado CO headed up the Operations Group.'

Sparrow's remit was to provide 24-hour cover to the C-TBM mission.

TF-20 AND C-TBM

In the early hours of 20 March, the 410th AEW flew its first OIF sorties. Sparrow struck a radio relay station with GBU-12s, but was dogged by fuel shortages when his tanker failed to show. Another flight had an even tougher time of it. With engines running and ready to taxi, the four-ship was re-tasked on the ground to hit an SA-3 SAM. The Vipers attempted to locate their tanker prior to 'crossing the fence', but this too proved impossible to find. As the sun came up, the flight experienced various equipment malfunctions, but pressed on to the target regardless, only to be called up by the RAF's "Bondo" AWACS controller, who told them to abort just at the point of bomb release!

Still carrying their bombs, and with their fuel already critically short, the flight was once again unable to find their outward bound support tanker. Nearing flame-out, the flight lead was calling over the radio for AWACS to provide vectors to the nearest available divert field, but got no reply. With the urgency of the calls increasing, and the radio calls nearing panic, an F-15E crewmember finally transmitted the coordinates of a hitherto unheard of airfield that was the Vipers' only option.

Without any tower or approach frequency to contact, the four F-16s finally made it down with only fumes to spare. They soon discovered that they had landed at a closed Saudi Arabian airfield that was being used as a logistics staging area and supply helicopter base for the troops in battle. Out of the early morning sun strode a young US Army trooper who instantly recognised the jets' 'AL' tail codes – by coincidence, he had previously been an F-16 crew chief for the 160th FS/180th FW at Montgomery, Alabama, no less! He was able to refuel the jets and ready them for their return flight to Azraq. Lady luck surely was on their side.

Despite all the C-TBM planning, the first day did not go as expected. According to Sparrow, 'the SOF guys on the ground immediately started calling for support, screaming that they were being attacked. For all our planning, no one had expected that we'd be providing all that much emergency CAS. We now had to decide whether we would stay up with our weapons at 20,000 ft and keep looking for Scuds, or say "screw that!" and roll in to help these guys on the ground, who sometimes were, no shit, fighting for their lives'.

According to Sparrow, it soon became obvious to the wing that there were no Scuds in the area – a sentiment backed-up by Maj Wolf's recollection that not a single TBM would be sighted by the 410th AEW throughout the entire war. Striking the right balance was critical, for if a Scud was launched while the Vipers were helping out SOF troops on the ground who were not in immediate danger, then there would be hell to pay, and people would be relieved of command.

Each squadron had its own philosophy. Some were resolute that they should actually influence the war by supporting the guys on the ground, while others were keener to follow the CAOC's guidelines. As it turned out, supporting the TF-20 troops ultimately became the most important mission – militarily, if not politically – that the Alabama ANG Vipers would perform.

The initial 'standard' load-out for the Azraq F-16s was four slant-loaded GBU-12s, but the wing soon moved to a mix of a single GBU-31 and two slant-loaded GBU-12s. As time progressed, and GBU-12 stocks became critically low, Mk 82 500-lb dumb bombs were used instead, typically with airburst FMU-14 fuses. Whatever the ordnance load out, the Alabama Vipers had a unique capability amongst the F-16 community – their AAQ-28 Litening II targeting pods could be linked to SADL, allowing data from BUG-E to cue their pods directly to the targets seen by the SOF ground commanders.

But technology was not always the solution, as Lt Col Sparrow's second OIF sortie on the early morning of 21 March showed. Flying as 'Flash 13' (flight lead to Capt Tony Simmons, call-sign 'Flash 14'), he was in 'Flash' flight's second element. An hour into his vul time, 'we got one of those calls from "Bondo" where you could just tell that something was going on. His voice was high and he was in a hurry. "'Snap 320', contact immediately 'Cobra 25' on 'Green 17'", and he gave us a secure frequency to go to. We went off at 320 degrees, tapped in the coordinates for the location of "Cobra 25" and then flew the jet towards the green diamond in the HUD. We had about 80 miles to go, and we were making calls to "Cobra 25", but no-one was talking to us'.

Fifty miles from the coordinates, Sparrow could tell that his steer point diamond was settling over some clouds, 'and I'm going "son of a bitch!", because from 20,000 ft we didn't want to go below those clouds – we didn't know how low they went. This was an event that we'd discussed in our meetings beforehand. I was thinking about this when the SOF guys came over the radio, panicked and running. Their call went something like, "'Flash 13', this is 'Cobra 25', brrrrp brrrrp brrrrp", as gunfire erupted in the background. "We're taking fire from four enemy trucks", then more gunfire and screaming. This was not supposed to be happening!'

Taken by surprise, Sparrow took his flight lower and lower as he looked for a hole in the clouds.

'I saw a little hole and shot through it. From 7000 ft down to 3500 ft I was in cloud, but then we popped out into clear blue sky. I was way too low to counter anyone shooting at me, and I'd thought for a minute looking down that I did not want to go through that cloud. It took me forever to find the SOF guys, who had been separated into two groups by the enemy'.

'Cobra 25' was a foot patrol made up of six or seven SOF guys, and they had become separated from 'Cobra 25 Tango', which was a Listening Post/Observation Post. '"Cobra 25T" were forward of "Cobra 25" by a couple of clicks, and when I showed up they were just two guys who were less than a kilometre from these four white pick-up trucks that were full of Iraqis shooting at them. I had to get my eyes onto both "25" and "25T" before I could release, then I had to get eyes on the trucks, which blended into the featureless desert so well that it really sucked to try and find them.'

Sparrow spent ten minutes over the desert at 3000 ft, but fortuitously the previous night's mission to hit the radio relay station gave him an advantage;

'"Cobra 25T" started telling me where he was in relation to what he described as a stick-like figure in the distance. We needed a ground point for reference, and SADL has stopped working because we were too far from our flight lead – "Flash 11", whose jet contained the lead SADL radio – and we had fallen off the SADL "net". Finally, it dawned on me that "Cobra 25's" voice sounded familiar – they were on the same frequency as us, and I could hear them talking to each other. I thought to myself, "that sounds like the guy from yesterday".'

Quickly establishing that this was the same SOF team that directed them to drop on the radio relay station the night before, Sparrow used the remains of it as a point of reference, and managed to get his eyes onto 'Cobra 25' and '25T'.

'Having found the first vehicle, I flew back and "threw" my pod at them. I got clearance from "25" and "25T" and was now really nervous because I had to fly straight and level in order to drop my bomb accurately. I thought back to my days as an F-16 pilot in Germany, remembering the visual lay downs at 500 ft that we used to do. We had a six-second arming delay time, and I knew that if I went below 1000 ft my bomb would not arm. We hadn't done the figures for dropping through the cloud at that point, so the guys on the ground would have to lase it to the target themselves – it was the only option that I thought would work. If I knew then what I know now, I'd have gone up above the clouds and let "Cobra 25" lase it in.'

With the decision to drop from 1000 ft, Sparrow could either fly straight over the target or execute a turning manoeuvre level turn (TMLT) to avoid the bomb blast. 'But I didn't want to pull 5Gs for a TMLT or the pod might lose track of the target and the bomb would miss. I made the pass and blew the truck up, but the delivery raised a few eyebrows when I got back and there were a lot of people who criticised me for my decision.

'Following my direct hit, the SOF guys spotted some guys driving another truck behind a stone farmhouse in a compound. I manoeuvred to come in from a different direction – south to north – and I saw the compound. I got clearance to re-attack and drop a bomb from 3000 ft on the south wall of the compound. The bad guys were behind the north wall, though. I should have taken my time, but I was really keen to get my bombs off and get some altitude. Well, I blew the crap out of the south wall, and the bad guys started running and the truck drove wildly out of the compound. There was one guy running after the truck, and he must have been screaming "wait for me!".

'I came back around for a ten-degree low-angle, low-drag delivery, but I lost the truck and came through the pass dry. I re-attacked, and this time I hit the truck directly and bugged out east. Coming back in from the west, I strafed the truck and then said, "Okay, we've had enough of this". We knew the "Sprint" threat was over, and we were now really offensive.'

Below and bottom
This aircraft has a more typical OIF load-out of one GBU-31 JDAM (bottom photograph) and two GBU-12s in slant configuration – note the older type of seeker head. This photograph also gives a good view of the additional chaff/flare dispensers built into the rear section of the aircraft's underwing pylons (*160th FS via Scott Patten*)

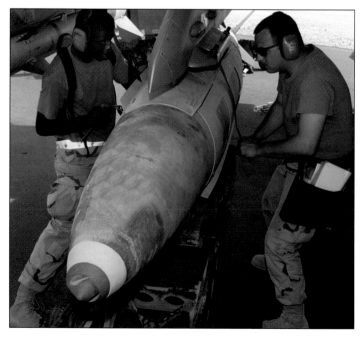

Climbing back up to 20,000 ft, 'Cobra 25' called 'Flash 13' and asked if he could neutralise one further truck. He agreed on the basis that it could be done from a safer altitude than before;

'I started a 45-degree dive and was slaloming around these clouds, trying to find a clear spot to put the bomb through. The truck was locked in the pod, and I eventually got the bomb off at around 7500 ft, travelling at what felt like Mach 2. It blew that truck up and I pulled out at about 3000 ft. Then we left. Back on the ground, my wingman gave me a "high five" and said "that was awesome!" "Yep!" I replied, "And I'm going to be grounded!"'

And so he was. Sparrow went straight to his CO and handed him his HUD tapes, resolved that he would have the tale straight from the source. Sparrow worked in the 'scheduling shop' for a few days before finally being allowed back into the jet.

BAATH PARTY HQ

The pace of operations for the first week was frantic, and the 410th AEW surged for its entirety. It left little time for meetings to dissect and analyse the missions being flown, their effect, or whether changes needed to be made. The wing was making good progress in the east, despite no Scud sightings, with all three Viper units providing air support for a Marines Corps force battling to capture Hadditha Dam. The latter was seen as strategically important because breaching it would cause mass flooding.

Unsurprisingly, the Marine Corps-led operation saw the Iraqi forces defeated, leading to a humorous exchange between the Marines and Iraqi PoWs. By all accounts, the Iraqis had been posted to the dam to prevent Coalition forces from destroying it, while the Marines, on the other hand, had been sent to the dam to prevent the Iraqis from destroying it!

In mid-March the 160th EFS received an experimental Operational Flight Program (OFP) which updated the Stores Management System in their jets. OFP SCU-5E was rushed into theatre and supported the delivery of JDAM, allowing the unit to move from slant loads of four GBU-12 to mixed loads of LGBs and JDAM. Combined with SADL, Litening II and JDAM, OFP SCU-5E provided the equipment synergy that was required to make C-TBM and TST missions more achievable.

In addition to the CAS and C-TBM work undertaken by the wing, there was also a smattering of pre-planned work to keep them busy. Lt Col Scott Patten (a 2900-hour Viper pilot who had flown 37 F-16 combat missions with the 69th TFS during Operation *Desert Storm* back in January 1991) flew a particularly memorable pre-planned strike against the Baath Party HQ in Al Quaem later in the war;

'Most of the stuff we were doing in OIF involved two-ship flights taking off with no assigned target(s), but my Al Quaem strike was one of the very few times that we knew we were going to go and hit pre-briefed aim points before we took off. I was the Ops Officer, and had treated the scheduling as fairly as I could, and it was therefore ironic that I ended up flying on this mission with 160th EFS CO, Col Karl Jones. I had been saying all along that we should fly together sometime, and on this particular day I had us down on the schedule to sortie as a pair, and the mission fell to us! Guys were coming up and saying that they couldn't believe we'd got one of the coolest missions of the war by accident.'

'For some reason, all the GBU-12s that were being dropped at around this time frame were all dropping short, and were therefore not as accurate as they should've been. When we first picked this mission up, Karl did not want to fly it – "No, if we screw this up as the squadron CO and Ops Officer, then how can we keep the young guys in check?".

'I told him that I'd lead the mission and do all the planning. I put everything else on hold and got to work trying to get to the bottom of the LGB issue. I found out that a lot of the inaccuracy was due to wind conditions – people were not taking tail winds and surface winds into account when bomb dropping. I was able to get hold of some SOF guys in the area and find out about the winds so I could plan this properly.'

Patten and Jones would have to execute a simultaneous release of two GBU-12s each, and split-second timing was everything as the former explained;

'All four had to hit within two seconds of each other. The target building was designed in two halves, and Karl was hitting one half and I was bombing the other.

'Taking off at midnight into atrocious weather, and a 7000-ft overcast, what was supposed to happen was that we would hit the building and an AC-130 in the target area would blow away anyone who scrambled out of it. However, when we got out there the weather was forcing everyone to hold in quite a small area, and I have to get special clearance to go below 10,000 ft to even see the target. It was rainy and misty, so I told my wingman and the AC-130 pilot that I was going to make a run at the target to see if we were going to be able to break it out. About five seconds before I pickled my LGB I saw the building. We flew back out and then ran in for real. We released, came off-target and the AC-130 told us over the radio that it was a good hit. There was nothing for them to clear up as the building has been demolished.

'By the time that we had landed, the word has already spread. We had people coming up to us saying, "Hey, you guys killed one of the high-priority generals and a couple of his lieutenants". At this point Al Quaem has not yet fallen, but it was taken the next day. Coalition troops in the area claimed that the town fell primarily because we took those leadership guys out. It was a big deal.'

466th FS F-16C 87-0338 sits bombed-up (with Mk 82s and GBU-12s) on the ramp between missions at Azraq. According to the 410th AEW's mission scheduler, Lt Col William Sparrow, there were as many as six different tail flashes on the ramp by the time OIF finally got underway on 20 March 2003 (*160th FS via Scott Patten*)

Patten returned to Al Quaem three days later, this time during the day;

'You could see where the building was, and where the monument right in front of it was. We had been very precise. The neighbourhood and the monument were completely untouched, but the Baath Party building had been levelled. No one was going to have gotten out of it.'

Patten received the DFC for his involvement in this key strike.

Col Clarke's Vipers – and the entire 410th AEW for that matter – had performed with alacrity. Between 19 March and 14 April, his F-16s had flown 1322 sorties for a total of 6504 hours flying time. During this period, the 160th EFS, augmented by personnel from the 121st FS, Washington DC ANG, conducted over 580 sorties (2822 hours, of which 1300 were with NVGs) and developed unique, innovative tactics to exploit Litening II and the Digital Network System Gateway for integration into the Coalition's expansive real-time intelligence, surveillance and reconnaissance network. This extraordinary feat represented the equivalent of nine months worth of normal peacetime flying, and allowed CENTCOM to assign the squadron a strategically significant mission that became the second highest priority in the OIF air campaign.

The wing dropped 518 GBU-12s, 24 Mk 82s and 89 GBU-31s. Of these, the 160th EFS accounted for 88 GBU-12s and 35 GBU-31s, leaving a trail of destruction that included over 50 tanks and APCs, countless troops, five fighter aircraft and 27 AAA pieces destroyed. The Alabama ANG finally returned home on 25 April 2003.

And what of the two M Sqn, Special Boat Service, soldiers that went missing the night Linch and Wolf provided them – and 52 of their colleagues – with CAS? Capt Brian Wolf explained;

'For three months I asked every day what happened to the two soldiers left behind, and the day before we were getting ready to leave, the British SOF liaison guy told me that they were alive and well in Syria! It was a great feeling to know, with hindsight, that we'd played a role in keeping them alive – we were the only guys within earshot to help them, and that's just another example of sheer luck. But for me and my flight lead, we didn't do enough. We not only wanted to save the guys on the ground, but also to kill the guys who were attacking them.'

187th FW CO Col Stanley Clarke prepares to taxi out from the ANG ramp at Montgomery Regional Airport at the start of a peacetime sortie in February 2005 (*FJPhotography.com*)

Maj Brian Wolf preps his jet prior to departing for the Nellis ranges to drop an inert GBU-31. This photograph highlights faded GBU-12 markings beneath the cockpit from the wing's 2003 deployment to Azraq (*FJPhotography.com*)

POST-SHOOTING WAR

With the entry of US troops into Baghdad came the final nail in the coffin for Saddam Hussein's ruthless dictatorship. The Coalition's rapid advance into the heart of Iraq had occurred with greater speed than many had thought possible, and gaining control of the Iraqi capital signalled to the rest of the country that bearing arms in defence of Saddam Hussein was no longer necessary. In the short-term the F-16s of the 410th, 332nd and 363rd AEWs flew fewer sorties and expended less ordnance, and all were eventually stood down and readied for a triumphant return home. Not a single F-16 had been lost.

At the time of writing, OIF remains very much in effect, and a host of Viper units have returned in support of it. The nature of their role in Iraq has shifted significantly from fighting uniform-clad Iraqi Army conscripts and regular soldiers, to supporting the Coalition (and the new Iraqi security forces) in a bid to neutralise the largely-invisible insurgency that has filled the power vacuum.

NTISR has taken on even greater importance in the three years that have passed since OIF I came to its natural conclusion. So too have the Urban CAS, Emergency CAS and TST roles, and F-16 pilots with recent experience in Iraq claim that they are closer than ever to entering the

In February 2004 the 107th FS, Michigan ANG, became the first F-16 unit to be stationed in Iraq. The squadron deployed to Kirkuk AB and remained in-theatre until June of that year. Since then, other units have also been based at Iraqi airfields, including Balad (*USAF*)

FAC(A) (Forward Air Controller (Airborne)) arena. In response to this changing and dynamic form of warfare, the F-16 continues to be equipped with leading-edge avionics, sensors and munitions.

History shows us that it is not only this forward thinking, but also open mindedness, that is essential if the F-16 is not only to survive, but to perform effectively. The NTISR sorties flown at the beginning of OIF may have irritated some, and the leaflet bombing sorties assigned to the 'Hounds' may have infuriated others, but as Maj Roberson explained, the value of these missions could not be underestimated.

Talk to ODS- and OIF-veteran Scott Patten and the change that the F-16's role has undergone over the last 15 years becomes immediately apparent. He recalls his Ops Officer in January 1991 telling a room full of 69th TFS Viper 'drivers' to look to the left and right of them, and to bear in mind that after their first mission over Iraq, one out of three pilots would not be returning home. Contrast that (thankfully) over-pessimistic estimate with the main concern of many Viper pilots the authors spoke to about their time over Iraq in 2003 – 'Please God, don't let me fuck it up!' – and the changing mindset becomes apparent.

SADL and the Fighter Data Link meant that F-16s operating in Iraq from March 2003 onwards were under the constant scrutiny of the CAOC, with their actions open to criticism almost before they had even taken place. This made the burden of responsibility feel heavier than ever before. The F-16 community has certainly felt that criticism at times – the release of pod video showing an F-16 pilot dropping a GBU-12 (at the request of the ground commander) on a group of insurgents in a street is one such example. The world's media grabbed the opportunity to second-guess the pilot by suggesting that he could not have known who they were, and to impugn this particular individual's integrity.

There have been successes, too, although these never make the world's headlines. Perhaps the most interesting story to have come out of Iraq since the shooting war ended comes from a familiar face. Maj Brian Wolf returned to OIF with the 160th EFS/187th FW – although this time flying from the more comfortable Al Udeid – in September 2004. There had been some speculation that the newest version of JDAM, the GBU-38, might soon arrive in-theatre. The GBU-38 had been hastily developed from the Mk 82 500-lb dumb bomb as a weapon eminently

F-16C 86-0328 of the 186th FS, Montana ANG, suffered a landing mishap at Balad AB on 11 July 2004 during the unit's deployment to Iraq. According to a report released by the Air Force soon after the incident occured, 'The aircraft was returning from a night close-air support mission when, on touchdown, a malfunctioning left brake caused the aircraft to pull right during the landing rollout and leave the runway. The aircraft hit an exposed concrete manhole cover with its nose landing gear and right main landing gear and came to rest 300 feet off the taxiway. Damage to the aircraft is estimated at $1.2 million' (*Scott Brown*)

85

suited to the Urban CAS mission. It used similar strap-on guidance and control kits as the 2000-lb GBU-31, but was far safer to use in the close confines of Iraqi cities and villages – the home of the insurgent.

It is perhaps more than a little ironic that Wolf's story forms the beginning of what was to become the battle for Falluja – a major drive to free the city from the insurgents hiding within – and was also the first-ever GBU-38 drop in combat, in an environment for which it was specifically designed. Wolf began;

'We got in-country and the load-out we were carrying was GBU-38 and slant loads of GBU-12s. We also had two AMRAAMs, 500 rounds of 20 mm and the AT Litening II pod. We were running oil pipeline routes looking for sabotage or leaks, and running "Crown Jewels", which were the power lines that people were wrecking to steal and sell the copper contacts.'

'Crown Jewel' and the pipeline patrols were ongoing at that time, and Wolf recalled that there was a constant flow of saboteurs;

'That night my wingman and I were on a three-hour vul, and late into the sortie. At about daybreak we got a call to contact the controlling agency, which we did. They asked us to go to secure radios and they then passed us coordinates, telling us, "we're going to need a TOT, run-in heading and read back of coordinates". We put the coordinates into the

Only cleared for frontline use in the Autumn of 2004, the arrival of the 500-lb GBU-38 in-theatre required additional software for the F-16's Stores Management Computer to be loaded into the Alabama ANG jets *in situ* at Al Udeid (*USAF*)

Carrying a mixed load-out of two slant-mounted GBU-12s and a single penetrator GBU-31(V)3/B, 134th FS, Vermont ANG, F-16C 85-0406 drops away from the tanker after refuelling over Iraq on 16 August 2004 (*USAF*)

jet and determined a good run-in heading based on winds. We were looking at the target complex with our Litening II pods – the FLIR was really good, and we could see the target from more than 20 miles away. We didn't want them to know we were inbound, so we stayed north of the target, which was in Falluja.'

The softening up of the city was just beginning, and a major drive to kill insurgent leader Abu Musab Zarqawi, was underway;

'By whatever means (I truly don't know), the troops on the ground had determined that there were Zarqawi operatives in this particular section of Falluja. In our targeting packs there were these DMPIs with commensurate coordinates on all of the safe houses and buildings in the area. They asked us if we had this specific DMPI in our packs, and we replied that we had because our Intel brief had covered them. They told us "look at the following DMPIs because they are potentially very high-

Also carrying a single GBU-31 (although of the more standard (V)1/B variety), this well-weathered 421st FS/366th FW jet was photographed at Balad in late 2004 during the height of the Falluja campaign (*Scott Brown*)

The youngest Viper assigned to the 119th FS, New Jersey ANG, F-16C 85-1411 streams condensation over its port wing as the pilot aggressively pulls the fully armed jet away from the tanker after inflight refuelling on 23 July 2005 (*USAF*)

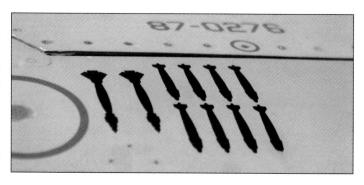

Fresh paint and the unmistakable silhouette of the GBU-38 identify these bomb markings on aircraft 87-0276 as being from the 187th FW's latest deployment to Iraq. This jet returned home to Alabama with a tally of eight GBU-38 and two GBU-12 drops to its credit (*FJPhotography.com*)

value targets", and they verified the coordinates. That was the critical thing to do with JDAM, even though we had DMPIs in our packs.

'When you're dropping JDAM we call it "O6 bombing", because even the colonels can hit the target. There are a few things to do before we drop – I have to cursor-zero my system to make sure there are no slews or errors in the navigation system, and I make sure I've got a GPS "High-High" guidance system because all that data is going to the JDAM.'

Wolf and his wingman held north of the target until they were satisfied with their plan, then they called their controlling agency and advised them they were inbound to the target;

'By now they had taken their Predator UAV and moved it away from the immediate area, but not too far away because they wanted to film and get BDA in real time back at the CAOC. We rolled in on-airspeed, on-heading and on-attack axis, and we reached the release parameters and hit the pickle button. There was a little dip in the wing as the cartridges fired, and I was now 500 lbs lighter on station 7 on the right wing. I checked left and put the pod in a good position to film some BDA, waiting the approximate 35 seconds until the bomb impacts. The building just shacked – two bombs put onto the same DMPI where they had assessed that there were Zarqawi operatives. At this point the sun was just starting to come up, and I put away the NVGs. It was a distinct and exact impact, and the bombs had hit within a second of each other.'

Wolf and his wingman, 'Rocky', went off-target and circled around for BDA. 'We picked up in our orbit in case they need more help, and as we were spinning, I got the distinct impression that it was "Shark Week" on The Discovery Channel! There was an F/A-18 circling above us, two more were below us and not too far away were a pair of F-16s. Word had obviously gotten out, because it was like sharks converging for the kill'.

Still unaware that they were the first to drop the GBU-38 in combat, Wolf and his wingman were cleared to return to Al Udeid;

'When we got home, the most surreal thing was debriefing – watching our tapes on huge black and white screens versus our small MFD. The GBU-38 had only taken out the target building, leaving the walls of the buildings on either side completely untouched.'

Moving to the chow hall at Al Udeid, the two sat down to omelette, hash browns and bacon in front of one of the giant TV screens;

'We heard Fox News talking about Coalition forces attacking Falluja early in the morning, and they showed the building reduced to rubble. We look at each other and smiled. "Hey dude, that was us!".

'We watched our tapes one more time on the big screen, and you could see just seconds before impact the two guys on the wanted list step out from the overhang of the building. They came walking out and you could see them in the FLIR picture. One guy took a drag off of a cigarette and you could see the heat from it. As he took it out of his mouth the bomb impacted and the war ended for him. We went home and got chow.'

F-16 VIPER UNITS OF OSW/OIF 2002-2005

Unit	Deployment Date(s)	F-16 build block	Unit	Date	F-16 build block
466th FS	December 2002 to May 2003	block 30	134th FS	2004	block 25
524th FS	December 2002 to May 2003	block 40	421st FS	June 2004	block 40
113th FS	2003	block 30	188th FS	July 2004	block 30
160th FS	February to May 2003	block 30	186th FS	July 2004	block 30
120th FS	February to May 2003	block 30	163rd FS	August to September 2004	block 25
157th FS	February to May 2003	block 52	555th FS	September to December 2004	block 40
22nd FS	February to May 2003	block 50	160th FS	September to December 2004	block 30
23rd FS	February to May 2003	block 50	170th FS	November 2004	block 30
13th FS	February to May 2003	block 50	421st FS	November 2004 to January 2005	block 40
14th FS	February to May 2003	block 50	34th FS	January to April 2005	block 40
77th FS	February to April 2003	block 50	4th FS	January to May 2005	block 40
421st FS	May to September 2003	block 40	112th FS	May to June 2005	block 42
175th FS	September 2003	block 30	124th FS	May to June 2005	block 42
149th FS	September to November 2003	block 30	125th FS	May to June 2005	block 42
510th FS	December 2003 to March 2004	block 40	179th FS	May to July 2005	block 25
555th FS	December 2003 to March 2004	block 40	119th FS	July 2005	block 30
107th FS	February to June 2004	block 30	510th FS	July to September 2005	block 40
457th FS	March to May 2004	block 30	555th FS	September to December 2005	block 40
466th FS	2004	block 30	93rd FS	September to December 2005	block 30

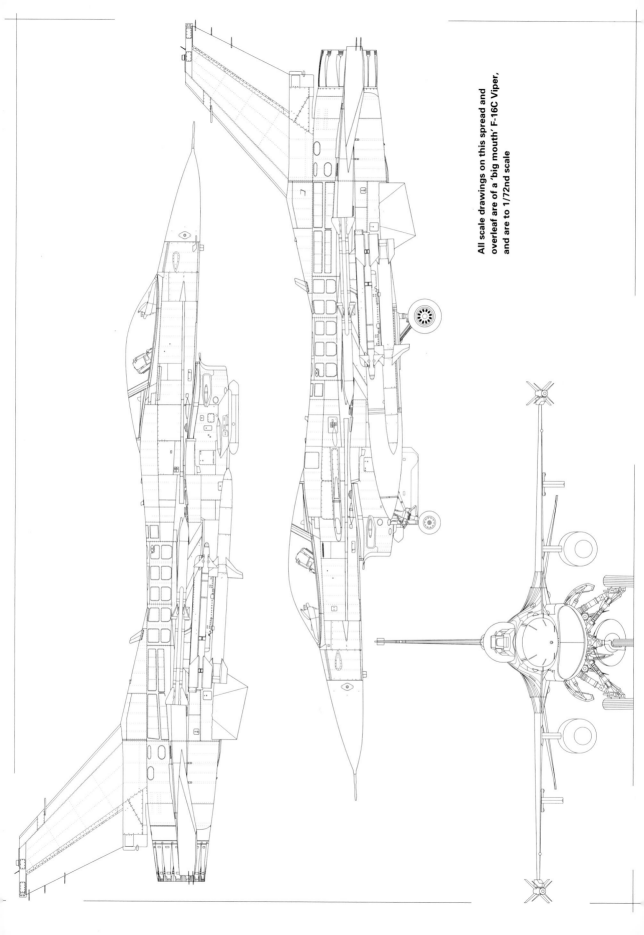

All scale drawings on this spread and overleaf are of a 'big mouth' F-16C Viper, and are to 1/72nd scale

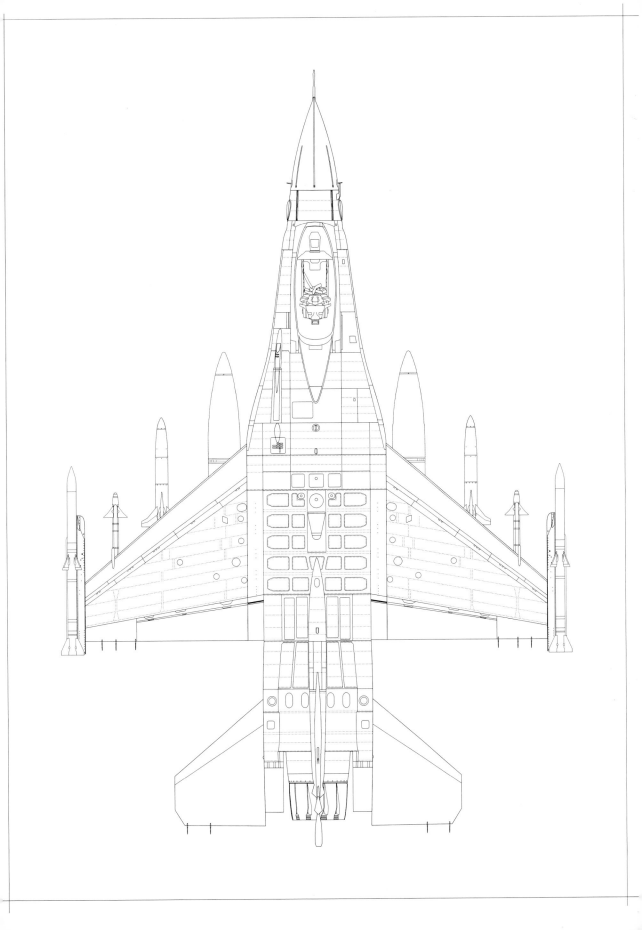

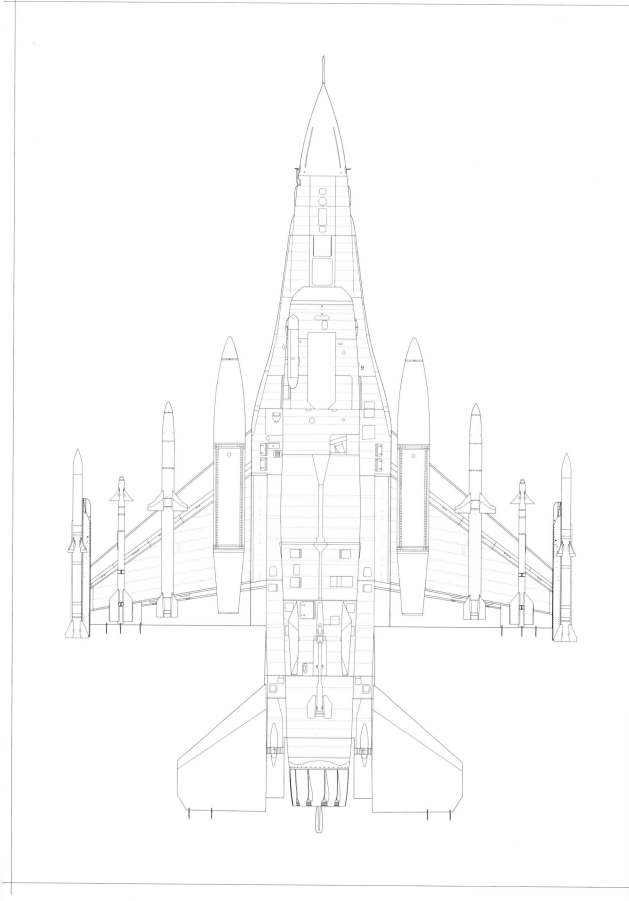

COLOUR PLATES

1

F-16C 87-0338 of the 466th FS/410th AEW, Azraq AB, Jordan, March 2003

This F-16C Block 30 was delivered to the USAF on 26 April 1989 and was accepted into the 63rd Tactical Fighter Training Squadron (TFTS) inventory in June of that year. The jet remained with the squadron – renamed the 63rd FS in October 1991 – until it moved to the 52nd FW at Spangdahlem AB, Germany. In January 1994 87-0338 was transferred to the 138th FS, before being assigned to the 466th FS/419th FW at Hill AFB, Utah, three months' later. It remains with the 'Diamondbacks' at time of writing, and is seen here carrying two low-drag general-purpose (LDGP) 500-lb Mk 82 bombs. This airframe carries the Lockheed Martin identifier 5C-599.

2

F-16C 91-0348 of the 77th FS/363rd AEW, Prince Sultan AB, Saudi Arabia, March 2003

Manufactured by General Dynamics as CC-46, this F-16CJ Block 50 was delivered to the USAF on 18 August 1993. The following month the fighter was flown to Germany, where it served with the 52nd FW at Spangdahlem AB. Its stay at 'Spang' was to be brief, however, and in June 1994 the jet was assigned to the 77th FS/20th FW at Shaw AFB. Depicted here wearing the standard 'Gamblers' markings, it carries two CBU-103 Wind Corrected Munitions Dispensers beneath its left wing.

3

F-16C 88-0528 of the 524th FS/332nd AEW, Al Jaber AB, Kuwait, March 2003

The most active Viper in the 'Hounds'' inventory during OIF, this General Dynamics-manufactured Block 40D airframe (construction number 1C-130) was originally delivered to the 69th TFS 'Werewolves' of the 347th FW at Moody AFB, Georgia, in May 1990. During the 2000 USAF base realignment, this unit was deactivated and 88-0528 transferred to the 524th FS/27th FW at Cannon AFB, New Mexico, in May 2001. Deploying to 'The Jaber' with the 'Hounds', the jet flew 44 bombing missions, including attacks against the Baath Party headquarters in Karbala. It is depicted here carrying its standard air-to-air load, as well as a pair of GPS-guided 2000-lb GBU-31 JDAM. These have a standard Mk 84 bomb body sheathed in a metal sleeve to prevent the casing from breaking up as it impacts hardened concrete.

4

F-16C 90-0776 of the 524th FS/332nd AEW, Al Jaber AB, Kuwait, March 2003

Built by General Dynamics as 1C-384, this Block 40K Viper was delivered to the 74th FS 'Flying Tigers' of the 23rd Composite Wing at Pope AFB, North Carolina, in February 1993. The unit was disbanded

about the same time that the 27th FW at Cannon AFB converted from its aged F-111D/Fs to F-16C/Ds, and 90-0776 was transferred to the 524th FS in July 1996. Since then it has been the squadron 'flagship', and the personal mount of 'Hound One' for a string of notable squadron commanders, culminating with Lt Col Tom Berghoff during OIF.

5

F-16C 94-0042 of the 77th FS/363rd AEW, Prince Sultan AB, Saudi Arabia, March 2003

Carrying the standard load seen during the opening days of the war, this 'Gamblers' F-16CJ Block 50 totes an AGM-88 HARM under each wing, and AIM-9M-9 and AIM-120B AMRAAM missiles for self-defence. CC-194 was built by Lockheed Martin in July 1996 and delivered directly to the 20th FW three months later. It remains a part of the 77th FS's inventory at time of writing.

6

F-16C 92-0920 of the 77th FS/363rd AEW, Prince Sultan AB, Saudi Arabia, March 2003

On 9 June 1995 CC-162 was issued to the USAF's 78th FS at Shaw AFB, but only after its entire left wing assembly had been replaced following the discovery of defective fuel lines during the acceptance inspection. Since then, this Block 50 F-16C has been transferred to the 77th FS, also at Shaw. Painted up as 20th FW Wing flagship during 2003, it has been nicknamed *Babygirl* by its crew chief and carries *Sumter/The Gamecock City* artwork behind the canopy. The tail flash is made up of squadron colours associated with the 20th FW's three F-16CJ units – the 55th, 77th and 78th FSs. The 70th FS 'Bushmasters' badge (formerly an F-16C/D then A-10 squadron) is featured on the jet's intake cheek, along with the three other squadron patches. Although officially deactivated in 1999, the 70th FS badge is carried for honours and lineage purposes.

7

F-16C 87-0254 of the 120th FS/410th AEW, Azraq AB, Jordan, March 2003

Another F-16C Block 30 manufactured by General Dynamics (as 5C-515), this Viper of the Colorado ANG has a USAF history that goes back to its entry into service with the 62nd TFTS in August 1988. One of the handful of 'Mile High Militia' jets that supplemented the Alabama ANG at Azraq AB, it carries a GBU-31 JDAM beneath its port wing. Note the additional ALE-47 counter munitions dispensers built into the pylon to which the JDAM is mounted.

8

F-16C 93-0541 of the 389th FS/379th AEW, Al Udeid AB, Qatar, March 2003

Although not widely-reported, the 389th FS/366th FW of Mountain Home AFB, Idaho, provided two

F-16CJ Block 52s to the 379th AEW to cover the absence of South Carolina ANG Vipers that were being upgraded as part of the Common Configuration Implementation Program (CCIP). The latter provides significant avionics upgrades to Block 40/50 F-16s, ensuring their state-of-the-art capability well into the 21st century.The aircraft deployed were the one shown and AF 91-0370. 93-0541 returned home with six AGM-88 and 14 Mk 82 silhouettes beneath its cockpit, whilst 91-0370 had two and four, respectively. 93-0541 (CC-176) entered service at Mountain Home AFB in March 1995.

9
F-16C 91-0417 of the 23rd FS/379th AEW, Al Udeid AB, Qatar, March 2003
Block 50 F-16C CC-115, built by General Dynamics, entered service with the 23rd FS/52nd FW at Spangdahlem AB in March 1994. It is depicted here wearing standard unit markings during OIF, the 'SP' tail codes denoting its 'Spang' home base. In 2004 the squadron's F-16s commenced their CCIP upgrade, and as part of the latter 91-0417 received an AAQ-14 targeting pod in 2005.

10
F-16C 90-0813 of the 22nd FS/379th AEW, Al Udeid AB, Qatar, March 2003
Entering service with the 22nd FS 'Stingers' in August 1993, F-16C Block 50 CC-13 has a GBU-31 JDAM and pair of AIM-120B AMRAAM missiles affixed to its right wing pylons. The F-16's self-defence fit of AIM-120 and AIM-9 missiles was varied throughout OIF, some jets featuring both types and others utilising one missile or the other exclusively. Note the aircraft's ASQ-213 HARM Targeting System (HTS) pod on its intake cheek.

11
F-16C 92-3886 of the 13th FS/363rd AEW, Prince Sultan AB, Saudi Arabia, March 2003
Block 50 F-16C CC-128 was delivered to the Air Force by Lockheed Martin in April 1994 and issued to the 13th FS/35th FW at Misawa AB, Japan. Still serving with this unit today, the jet features the prestigious 'WW' tail codes of 'Wild Weasel' fame on its fin. Two external fuel tanks were carried on all Viper missions during OIF, and the presence of an AGM-88 HARM on the left wing shows the aircraft armed with an early-war load-out.

12
F-16C 91-0399 of the 13th FS/363rd AEW, Prince Sultan AB, Saudi Arabia, March 2003
Another Block 50 Viper that has served exclusively with the 13th FS since new, 91-0339 is depicted here carrying an AGM-65E Laser Maverick air-to-ground missile. The LMAV proved to be a useful SEAD tool during OIF, the missile being widely used after it became clear that the Iraqi IADS was not going to activate its radars, thus denying the F-16CJs' ability to target them with HARM. The AGM-65 allowed precise visual targeting from

relatively safe stand-off distances. 91-0399 (CC-97) was delivered to Misawa in January 1994.

13
F-16C 93-0537 of the 157th FS/379th AEW, Al Udeid AB, Qatar, March 2003
The 'Swamp Foxes' of the169th FW, South Carolina ANG, deployed to Al Udeid with their Block 52s to support the SEAD/DEAD effort planned for OIF. This aircraft (CC-172) was built by Lockheed Martin in December 1994, and has been with the 157th FS since new. It has been nicknamed *Gamecock* by its groundcrew.

14
F-16C 87-0336 of the 160th FS/410th AEW, Azraq AB, Jordan, March 2003
Block 30 F-16C 5C-597 was delivered to the USAF by General Dynamics in May 1989, and it was subsequently sent to Spangdahlem AB for service with the 23rd TFS/52nd TFW. Remaining in Germany until December 1993, the aircraft was then assigned to the 160th FS/187th FW, Alabama ANG. As with all Alabama Vipers, it is named after one of the state's cities, in this case Enterprise. 87-0336 returned home with 18 OIF mission markings (17 GBU-12 and one JDAM), which were added to two GBU-12 silhouettes from a previous Operation *Northern Watch* deployment. This jet is nicknamed *Little Miss* (written beneath the RWR blister behind the radome on the right side only), and it also boasts the letters *RIO* in red on the inside of the nose landing gear door. The city name on the tail was removed during OIF and then reapplied post-war.

15
F-16C 86-0341 of the 160th FS/379th AEW, Al Udeid AB, Qatar, June-August 2004
5C-447 was delivered new to the 613th TFS at Torejon AB, Spain, in April 1988. It subsequently joined the 52nd FW at Spangdahlem AB in 1991, and then entered ANG service with 170th FS at Springfield, Illinois, in 1993. Passed on to the Alabama ANG in June 2004, the Block 30 Viper is depicted here wearing the low-conspicuity markings adopted by the 160th FS prior to the unit's return to Iraq in June 2004. Seen here carrying GBU-12 500-lb LGBs, the jet presently wears high-conspicuity 'Tuskegee Airmen' commemorative markings that include a bright red vertical tail.

16
F-16C 87-0263 of the 160th FS/410th AEW, Azraq AB, Jordan, March 2003
Alabama ANG jets often sortied with a mixed load of GBU-31 JDAM and GBU-12s, as seen here, in OIF. The LGBs were carried as 'slant loads' on a Triple Ejector Rack . This F-16C Block 30 served with the 63rd TFTS upon delivery to the USAF in November 1988, and it was later assigned to the 52nd FW at Spangdahlem AB. It returned to the US in December 1993 when it was tranferred to

the 160th FS/187th FW at Montgomery Field. The jet's General Dynamics identifier is 5C-524. The fighter's AAQ-28 Litening II targeting pod was carried on the right-hand side of the intake cheek.

17
F-16C 91-0336 of the 22nd FS/379th AEW, Al Udeid AB, Qatar, March 2003
Delivered new to the 22nd FS/52nd FW at Spangdahlem AB in June 1993, General Dynamics airframe CC-34 has been utilised exclusively by this unit for the past 12 years. The 52nd FW consists of two F-16CJ Block 50 Viper units (the other unit is the 23rd FS) and a single squadron of A-10 Thunderbolt IIs. Initially earmarked to fly out of Incirlik AB, Turkey, for OIF, both of the 52nd FW's F-16CJ squadrons were reassigned to Al Udeid when diplomatic negotiations to host the aircraft in Turkey ended in failure. The 81st FS's A-10s remained in Germany for the duration of the war as a result of these basing problems.

18
F-16C 90-0829 of the 22nd FS/379th AEW, Al Udeid AB, Qatar, March 2003
90-0829 has also served with the 22nd FS/52nd FW since its delivery to the USAF in June 1993. Built by General Dynamics as CC-29 in May 1993, it has worn mission markings from a range of operations, including *Northern Watch*, *Southern Watch* and *Iraqi Freedom*. The fighter was designated the 22nd FS flagship in 1998, but since OIF it has been repainted in standard 'Stinger' markings.

19
F-16C 85-1402 of the 457th FS/379th AEW, Al Udeid AB, Qatar, March-May 2004
Wearing the characteristic 'TX' tail codes of the Fort Worth-based 457th FS/301st FW, this F-16C Block 30 carries a pair of GBU-38 500-lb JDAM as a slant load beneath its left wing. The GBU-38 provides a more suitable option for Urban Close Air Support on account of its smaller lethal 'footprint' – it was actually dropped in anger for the first time by a 160th FS F-16C Block 30. This Viper (5C-182) entered the USAF inventory in November 1986 with the 526th TFS, then moved to the 506th FS in the mid-1990s and was eventually assigned to the 425th FS in April 1997.

20
F-16C 91-0345 of the 77th FS/363rd AEW, Prince Sultan AB, Saudi Arabia, March 2003
Serving in Germany with Spangdahlem's 22nd FS from September 1993 until February 1994, this Block 50 F-16C has since been assigned to the 55th FS and, latterly, the 77th FS/20th FW. Built by General Dynamics as CC-43, it is depicted here wearing the mission markings from its participation in OIF. As with all the F-16 profiles in in this book, it carries the centrally-mounted ALQ-131(V)-14 electronic jamming pod and, in common with all Block 50/52 Vipers that went to OIF, boasts an ALE-50 towed-array decoy device integrated into the No 2 pylon.

21
F-16C 88-0416 of the 524th FS/332nd AEW, Al Jaber AB, Kuwait, March 2003
An early Block 40 jet, this Viper was built by General Dynamics as 1C-18 and first assigned to the 34th TFS 'Rude Rams' as part of the 388th FW at Hill AFB. Transferred to the 524th in October 1996 as part of the unit's conversion from F-111s to F-16s, it was one of the original 'Hound' jets to deploy to Al Jaber on 18 December 2002. The aircraft flew some 22 bomb-dropping missions and is depicted here late in the conflict carrying a pair of 'bunker-busting' 2000-lb GBU-24 LGBs. These were used by the 'Hounds' to destroy IrAF MiG fighters found buried in the desert.

22
F-16C 90-0756 of the 524th FS/332nd AEW, Al Jaber AB, Kuwait, March 2003
A late Block 40 jet, 90-0756 was completed by General Dynamics as 1C-364 and initially joined Shaw's 363rd FW in July 1992, before being assigned to the 68th FS 'Lightning Lancers' of the 347th FW at Moody AFB one year later. When that unit was disbanded, the jet was transferred to the 524th FS in April 2001. It too was one of the F-16s sent on the unit's initial AEF VII deployment to Kuwait in December 2002, but it was not as heavily flown as other 'Hounds' mounts. It is shown here late in OIF, with only a pair of GBU-12 bombs aboard. Usually slant loaded one pair per wing, the unit had to go on 'half rations' because so many of these surgical weapons had been used that stocks were running low by the end of OIF.

23
F-16C 90-0818 of the 22nd FS/379th AEW, Al Udeid AB, Qatar, March 2003
CC-18 is another Block 50 F-16C that went straight from General Dynamics into the 52nd FW's inventory in Germany, arriving at Spangdahlem AB in February 1993. Assigned to the 22nd FS ever since, this aircraft experienced a minor in-flight fire in the mid-1990s when water in station No 5's cannon plugs caused a short circuit, but the jet was returned to base safely without further ado.

24
F-16C 96-0080 of the 23rd FS/379th AEW, Al Udeid AB, Qatar, March 2003
CC-202 was delivered to the USAF by Lockheed Martin in June 1999, and it was in turn sent to the 23rd FS/52nd FW at Spangdahlem AB, less than a month later. The aircraft has since been bestowed the honour of being the 23rd FS's flagship, and was formerly painted in the stylised squadron colours seen here. Since its return from OIF, the Block 50 Viper has been repainted in a slightly more formal flagship scheme.

INDEX

References to illustrations are shown in **bold**. Plates are shown with page and caption locators in brackets.